Jeremiah Goodman, who had a famous career as an illustrator for
Vogue and other fashion publications, as well as being a painter
in his own right, executed dazzling expressionistic paintings of
Rose's living room (shown) and bedroom (page 212).
Painting, by Jeremiah Goodman, courtesy of Dean Morgan.

If you were to ask me the overall thing about Rose Cumming, I think I would say she was totally, incredibly unusual. Every now and then someone comes along who goes beyond training, background, or whatever and they have this mysterious talent and that places them with "the best" — whoever judges things. Some of them have an extra bite that makes them really special. It's a sense of drama. Rose Cumming's talent was like Garbo's face.

Jeremiah Goodman, artist

Rose Cumming at her most regal in the 1930s. She sent this studio portrait to her nephew, Tony Cumming, inscribed "From Rose, with my fondest love, my darling Tony." *Courtesy of Anthony Cumming.*

ROSE CUMMING

DESIGN INSPIRATION

DESSIN FOURNIR
COLLECTIONS

WRITTEN BY
JEFFREY SIMPSON

FOREWORD BY
SARAH CUMMING CECIL

RIZZOLI
NEW YORK

New York · Paris · London · Milan

First published in the United States of America in 2012 by

RIZZOLI INTERNATIONAL PUBLICATIONS, INC.
300 Park Avenue South, New York, NY 10010 www.rizzoliusa.com

© 2012 Rizzoli International Publications, Inc.
© 2012 DFC Holdings LLC

2012   2013   2014   2015   2016   2017 / 10 9 8 7 6 5 4 3 2 1

Distributed to the U.S. Trade by Random House, New York

Designed by Scott J. Gross

Printed and bound in China

ISBN-13: 978-0-8478-3846-2
Library of Congress Control Number: 2012935259

PHOTOGRAPHY CREDITS
The publisher and author have done everything possible to clear permissions for images used in this book. If a credit is incorrect or missing inadvertently, the publisher, if notified of this omission, will correct such credits in future printings of the book.

ENDPAPERS
De Gournay's hand-painted *Jardinières & Citrus Trees*, courtesy of de Gournay.

INTRODUCTORY IMAGE
Rose Cumming, in writing about her house, said of the sleigh of which this beast is the figurehead, "An extraordinary sleigh of the Regence [1715–1728], made in Alsace-Lorraine ... for Stanislas Lescinsky, the father-in-law of Louis XV." And then, being Rose, she added, "Perhaps the most distinguished example of its kind in the country." Photograph by Iva Batistic, courtesy of Carlton Hobbs, LLC.

TABLE OF
CONTENTS

ABOVE Rose (left) and her sister Eileen Cumming Cecil
with Eileen's grandchildren. The coromandel screen,
originally chosen by Rose, was a fixture in all of Eileen's
residences. *Courtesy of Sarah Cumming Cecil.*

FOREWORD

SARAH CUMMING CECIL

Few people remain on earth who knew Rose Cumming. I began researching my great-aunt's life with vigor in 1986 after I was approached by the Cooper Hewitt Museum to give a talk about her as part of a daylong program they were presenting entitled Legends of Design. I had been living in New York, writing on fashion, art, antiques, and interior design for several years, while working at Rose Cumming, Inc. When I got the call to speak, I had just left New York and moved to Maine to marry. I leapt at the chance to give the talk, despite a terror of public speaking, as thus far I had found neither work nor friends in Maine. Thankfully, I got past my shyness, presented the program, and have since gone on to give the illustrated talk at many other institutions while continuing my Cumming family research and interior design work.

In 1978, between stints as a freelance writer, I cut my editorial teeth when I took a job as the editor's assistant at *Antiques World*, a magazine the venerable *ARTnews* was launching. It was there that I first encountered Jeffrey Simpson, who, several years my senior and with that much more editorial experience behind him, was soon hired as a senior editor. Jeffrey became a friend. Then, as I moved on, we lost touch. Our writing, however, continued to cross paths in the pages of various magazines. We serendipitously reconnected on this book project last year.

Just as people change their behavior for different audiences and interactions so do people's perceptions vary. It is these contradictions that make the task of writing a biography both challenging and endlessly interesting.

Rose and her two sisters, Dorothy and my grandmother Eileen, were born in Australia. They grew up on a sheep ranch in Sydney. Inevitably, mention of an Australian sheep ranch upbringing makes some leap to the conclusion that

there are convicts in the family tree, as well as dust, dung, and poverty, but this is far from the case. My maternal great-grandparents, Victor and Sarah Cumming, were "proper Brits" (going so far as to forbid the girls from speaking with the Australian Cockney accent). From all reports, the girls had happy, socially engaged upper-class childhoods—the kind of turn-of-the-century Australian existence best illustrated by the 1979 Australian film *My Brilliant Career* after the heroine leaves the family farm and moves in with her urbane cousins and begins a rich, social whirl.

Given such blissful beginnings, it is intriguing that each of the Cumming girls gave up Australia for the United States as soon as she was old enough to book passage. The girls' upbringing, with its boundless support and love, encouraged a maverick spirit—and, with it, confidence. It is likely that their father, to a large degree, was influential. Victor Cumming was a bookish gentleman of leisure whose fascination with the statistics of gambling made for persistently shaky finances. He regularly went to Monte Carlo, and his travels must have made the world seem like a smaller place, erasing the isolation of Australia while, at the same time, making the girls aware of its remoteness. This instability may have encouraged the girls to think in terms of securing independence and careers—as well as giving them a taste for risk.

One by one, in quick succession, the girls crossed the world and came to America. Dorothy, the youngest, was the first to arrive in the United States. She headed to Hollywood, quickly landing a staring role as the Virgin Mary in Cecil B. DeMille's classic *King of Kings*. Rose was next. She was followed by my grandmother Eileen, who became a prominent advertising executive and editor at *Vogue* and *Harpers Bazaar*. My great-grandparents followed in quick order, and moved in with Rose and Eileen. The Cumming roost was now officially transplanted.

By all accounts, Rose was a remarkable beauty. (My fraternal grandfather, Dr. Russell Cecil, first encountered the Cumming clan when he visited their New York apartment to take Rose out, bewitched by her beauty—though it was my grandmother, Eileen, who won his heart.) Rose never married but evidence suggests she did not lack for admirers and marriage opportunities, and speculative stories about her romantic life abound. My grandmother was the first to defend her virtue, most notably in response to a 1979 *New York Times* story that referenced a putative liaison with the married financier Otto Kahn. I remember huddling around the old Olivetti in the shop, taking dictation from my enraged grandmother, and typing out the letter onto the small square sheets of her blue Merrimade stationery. (The *Times* ran my grandmother's response in full.) Rose's delight in décolleté and in calling herself "The Virgin Queen," however, was hardly the behavior of an uptight spinster.

As a child, I made regular visits to the shop to see Aunt Rose. Not a bad thing because it ensured a stop at FAO Schwartz, the great toy store around the corner, and there was always something strange and beautiful to check out at Aunt Rose's. She would sit at her desk, under a hat or wearing a crown of laurels or fern fronds in her tangled halo of blue hair. Occasionally, she would surprise me with a gift—beads or silk flowers—but for the most part she seemed remote.

I started working at the shop as a teenager in 1968, the year Rose died and my grandmother took over the business. To this day the family refers to the Rose Cumming business base as "the Shop," something that now seems quaint. But until it moved to its current address in the Fine Arts Building at 232 East Fifty-ninth Street, it was just that, a shop—ground floor, open to everyone, and something Rose was very proud of. It held several addresses over the years, most notably 515 Madison Avenue, near Fifty-third Street, 489 Park Avenue in the famous Anderson Galleries, and then finally 499 Park Avenue, in a small, wide, turn-of-the-century building on the corner of Park Avenue and Fifty-ninth Street, where we shared a longtime lease with the Catholic Church and where the tall I. M. Pei building now stands.

Rose made her reputation with the Madison Avenue shop, which was considerably larger than the later Park Avenue location. A duplex, it had a balcony offering a second floor of furniture for purchase, and the desk of Miss Fish, a small, Central European woman who handled the accounts for Rose for years.

As in her residences, Rose valued high ceilings and good light in her shop spaces. The story of her lighting the windows at night in the first shop is legend, and the windows were dominant and used for display. At 499 Park Avenue, they stretched from floor to ceiling, an expanse about 30 feet high. Within, the walls had a dark purple or aubergine glaze, giving the place a vaguely cavernous feel, which amplified an overall impression that one had entered a unique and magical place. A maze of chandeliers hanging overhead was reflected in a wall of distressed Venetian mirrors. The antiques were thoughtfully placed, but in a manner that suggested they had just landed there, lending a feeling of the imminent discovery of hidden treasures. The far wall consisted of shelves from which stacked bolts of fabric protruded, cockeyed with handwritten tags flapping from the ends of cardboard tubes. She hated electricity and only selectively used spotlights, avoiding floodlights that screamed "Don't miss this gem."

When the 499 Park Avenue building was sold unexpectedly in 1977, destined for demolition, the shop moved to the fourth floor of the Fine Arts Building, a to-the-trade-only edifice.

OPPOSITE Rose's mother's room, painted by Mark Hampton, was done in orchid, mauve and purple, with draperies of her famous delphinium print. *Watercolor, by Mark Hampton, courtesy of Duane Hampton.*

Thus began the transition to its current spotless showroom identity. No longer situated at street level and open to the public, its focus shifted to appeal to a less eclectic mix: decorators and the clients they had in tow.

During Rose's time, many young decorators felt emboldened to cross the shop's threshold and ask her to take them on as assistants, some with happier results than others. Tales of Rose's brutal honesty are balanced by stories of her generosity and kindness. Her staff at home adored her and stayed with her for years.

Rose's work ethic was legendary. Running a shop took up as much, if not more, of her time in later years than the decorating did. The late Richard Hare spoke of feeling elated as he reported for work the first day, only to be handed a broom and asked to clean out the basement.

Being at street level meant lots of flying dust and dried leaves, not to mention the occasional thief, but the boredom and dirty work of shop keeping was balanced by the influx of personalities who came through the doors. While working there as a teenager, I liked to lounge in the back of the shop, stretched out on the enormous marble "cutting table," which was layered with fine old rugs. One day, I had no sooner pronounced, "Oh my God, I am so bored. When is someone interesting going to walk in?" then there came the familiar tinkle of the shop bell and a cheery: "Hello Mrs. Cecil, it's Babe Paley and Gloria Guinness." The elegant visitors always politely announced themselves, as they entered the shop, and they often sat down to chat. Bottles of brandy were kept in the desk drawer for afternoon entertaining. Kay Thompson of *Eloise* fame was a great friend of both my aunt and grandmother's and came by often, as did Andy Warhol, Fred Hughes, and clients like Linda Ronstadt. As a young decorator, Tom Britt was a close friend of Rose's. His wife, Julie, was at *Harper's Bazaar* and, being handy with a needle and thread, would be called upon to add greater depth to the already plunging necklines of Rose's dresses. Mark Hampton, Albert Hadley, and Mario Buatta are just a few of the many decorators who have documented their interactions with Rose over the years. The first time Sister Parish entered the shop, rumor reports, Rose threw her out.

Rose had no patience for the predictable. If she didn't like a customer, she would tell him things were not for sale. The harmless standard "Just browsing," was met with a grim: "Cows browse."

It is remarkable to consider that Rose Cumming as well as her colleagues Syrie Maugham and Elsie de Wolfe, as pioneers of interior design, crossed continents with their decorating work, and operated shops that further established their reputations and design identities. These were brave, indomitable women who seemed to respect each other. Maugham and de Wolfe would travel together to India in 1936. Rose also interacted with the famously temperamental Maugham. When Maugham closed her New York shop in 1932 and someone suggested Rose fill the gap by designing white furniture after the model of Maugham, Rose immediately responded, "No. White was always Syrie's."

Rose's designs that I grew up with tend to reflect her passion for all things chinoiserie, with a nod to Chippendale. She loved lacquer and even had her Steinway grand piano lacquered in black to soften and deepen the standard sheen. She had a fondness for antiqued mirrored surfaces. She originated mixing high and low, valuing beauty over luxury. Even in the 1920s, at the height of the rumors of the "white slave trade" in New York's Chinatown, Rose loved to haunt the small shops there, often integrating what she found into her work, creating accessories for the home, including place mats, sconces, and side tables. To market these designs, she photographed them, providing a helpful reference.

It is unfortunate that more of her design projects weren't photographed—a fact made all the more mysterious by my grandmother's work as an editor at *Vogue* and *Harper's Bazaar*. One of the challenges in researching Rose is locating photographs. Of course, today everything is photographed so any archive pales by comparison.

One always wonders about the next wave. At this moment, the turn-of-the-twentieth-century minimalist phase, conceivably the result of new money that came out of the Internet explosion seems to be cooling. Meanwhile, interest in color and antiques, which have languished for the past decade or two, is picking up. Unlike the wannabe-Anglophile trend of the 1980s, the new interest is in the weird and decadent. Taxidermy and all things reptilian are hot and one cannot but recall Rose's incredible so-called "Ugly Room," with its Audubon prints of snakes and quadrupeds complemented by Moorish doors and fabrics. It is a testament that her designs remain timeless and striking.

At the heart of her unique design vision was eclecticism—the unexpected mixing of periods, patinas, shapes, and color—while creating rooms of extraordinary beauty. This book offers a window into her unusual rooms and life.

PROLOGUE

Rose Cumming was a legend in her own time—and like most legends she was both unique and tremendously appealing. In her old age, she presented the figure of a stylish bag lady—vivid purple hair, décolleté sacks for dresses ("Lower, dear, lower," she said about the neckline to a young friend who was helping to shape one of her garments), and huge picture hats in jewel tones. She did not suffer fools gladly—"I have no time for boring furniture, boring fabrics or boring people," she asserted—but a generation of mature decorators who have made the profession a national commodity in the last 30 years remember the painstaking kindness "Miss Rose" showed them as young men just arrived in New York or as undergraduates at the Parsons School of Design.

"She taught you about the provenance and workmanship of everything in her shop," says Albert Hadley, one of the principals of the renowned firm Parish Hadley. "I had just come from Tennessee in the 1940s, and that shop was the most magical place I had ever seen. And Miss Rose took you under her wing."

Indeed, Rose Cumming had a shop—that in her later years is what people knew about her and remember. On the corner of Fifty-third Street and Madison Avenue, it was a fantasy land of important French and English antiques cluttered with empty candy boxes and blue Bromo-Seltzer bottles from the drugstore that were also for sale. The sense of theater that informed Rose's life inspired her to put electric fans on the floor, aimed at the ceiling to set the chandeliers tinkling. At one time a sheet of water ran permanently down the side windows to keep the flowers fresh, and she always left the lights on all night, so that the beau monde walking home from dinner parties in their evening gowns and top hats could be tempted by the delights inside. There were also bolts of fabrics, wonderful chintzes colored by Rose and printed in England and France, from which she would cut widths with shears tied to the leg of a Louis XV desk with a length of white silk ribbon.

OPPOSITE A watercolor by the late Mark Hampton of Rose's drawing room. He says that it "captured the whimsical chinoiserie charm of a rococo pavilion in a palace garden." *Watercolor, by Mark Hampton, courtesy of Duane Hampton.*

The shop was in the European mode of being a retail antiques shop, the office for Rose's decorating business, and the center of a wholesale fabric business known as "To The Trade."

Rose, like the best artists, was self-created. Although she began her career when interior design—or decorating as it was known—was just beginning to be recognized and she studied with some of the most significant people in the business, she, as much as any of the early greats, on her own defined interior design as a profession and a form of artistic expression.

Like any artist, Rose went through periods of development. Her early public work for clients in the 1920s tended to be opulent but conventional. English portraits and antiques were made distinctive on backgrounds of eighteenth-century Chinese wallpaper. She established herself as a society figure. Accompanied by her longtime escort, a brilliantine-haired Italian count named Antonio Algara ("a 'no count' count," sniffed Old New York), her presence was noted again and again in the *New York Times* social pages: "Miss Rose Cumming entertains…"; "Mrs. Victor Cumming and her daughter, Miss Rose Cumming, of Southampton, have taken an apartment at the Plaza for the winter…"; "Miss Rose Cumming sails for Europe on the Berengaria…"

Rose opened her shop in 1921, and all of these social engagements were targeted to be sales calls, in effect, with potential clients enticed and, one hoped, committed to a decorating contract or at least a visit to the shop. Rose never did anything without a purpose; she lived by her wits and was a wandering minstrel of the visual and domestic arts, earning her livelihood by a constant display of her talent. Baron Adolphe de Meyer, one of the most fashionable photographers of the day, did a portrait of actress Genevieve Tobin in a Rose Cumming interior in *Vogue* as early as 1921; and, in 1932, Edward Steichen, the official photographer of Condé Nast from 1925 to 1937, did Rose's portrait, which also appeared in *Vogue*, her head with its nimbus of hair leaning pensively on an arm bedecked with bracelets and brocade.

Rose had been bankrolled in the shop by her sister, Dorothy Cumming Eliot (later McNab), the silent film star, and she went through a Hollywood period during which the names of Mary Pickford, Norma Shearer, and Gloria Swanson appeared in her address book.

In 1928, Rose published an article in *Arts & Decoration* magazine, "The Remaking of an Old Brownstone," and there in newsprint sepia are the fantastic Xanadu-like rooms of her house that would become her signature achievement.

The threads of Rose's life—the exhibitionism, the social climbing ("One Christmas the Duchess of Windsor bought all her gifts in Rose's shop," said her sister Eileen), the art and antiques dealing, and the decorating—all were means to an end: the self-expression of an artist whose media were colors and beautiful objects. Women like Elsie de Wolfe around the turn of the twentieth century had made decorating into the wrappings for a lifestyle. Rose went farther and created illusions, illusions that she inhabited and that she took you into.

She had acolytes, men who became famous in their profession such as Albert Hadley, Thomas Britt, Mario Buatta, Mark Hampton, and William Hodgins—acolytes but no heirs.

There was never anyone like Rose.
But it all had to start some place.

ACKNOWLEDGMENTS

I wish to thank Charles Comeau, president of Rose Cumming by Dessin Fournir and president and CEO of the Dessin Fournir Collections, for sharing his vision of what Rose Cumming meant to the history of design by facilitating the creation of this book. His unstinting support from the time of the first discussions about the book has allowed an invaluable part of design history to be preserved and to serve as inspiration for the future.

This book would not exist without the enthusiasm, professionalism, and dedication of Billie Ayers, Archivist of Rose Cumming by Dessin Fournir. Having imagined the book as a possibility for many years, it was she who sought out every scrap, literally, of information about Rose, from archival photographs in the unlikely files of The New-York Historical Society to a portrait of Rose that had been incorporated into the upholstery of a chair seat. I cannot express enough appreciation for her forbearance with my moods and doubts, while researching and writing the manuscript. Her meticulous preparation of the manuscript for publication was essential and exhaustive in every sense of the word.

I am very grateful to David Morton, associate publisher of Rizzoli International Publications, who saw the possibilities of this book from the beginning, and to Douglas Curran, editor, who worked hard to make the book a reality.

I wish to thank many people who generously gave of their time and their memories in extended interviews, which allowed Rose to come alive in the book.

Rose's nephew, the late Russell Cecil, and his wife, Nancy, offered personal memories back to the 1930s, not only of Rose, but also of her sisters, Eileen, who was Russell's mother, and Dorothy. On a number of chilly trips I made to Rye, New York, they kindly provided chicken sandwich lunches at which Rose was practically a fourth guest.

Albert Hadley, the dean of American interior design, opened his beautiful apartment to me on a number of occasions during which he plied me with cocktails and summoned up "Miss Rose" and her tutelage of him, when he first arrived in New York. His graphic and dramatic narratives re-created Rose and her spaces and her world as no one else could.

Thomas Britt, one of Rose's favorite protégés, freely exercised his photographic memory and took me through Rose's greatest creation, her house on West Fifty-third Street, missing no detail. It was Tom alone who remembered the renovation of Toots Shor's restaurant that knocked down Rose's garden wall and broke her Ming Foo dogs.

Iconic illustrator Jeremiah Goodman, who has painted Rose's interiors in explosive, expressionistic creations, opened my eyes to the specific nature of Rose's talent, such as her fondness for matching jewel tones with earth tones. "Nobody had ever done that, but jewels come out of the earth and they glitter," he said.

The irrepressible Mario Buatta took me through the vivid memories of his relationship with Rose, from helping her clean her house to taking her to the movies to the creation of her iconic "Ugly Room." "But it wasn't ugly," he said. "It was pretty, so she couldn't do ugly."

Bunny Williams, who knew Rose at the very end of her life, had perhaps a unique understanding of her as a woman making a career on her own, and helped me to see Rose from the inside, rather than as a performer. Her statement that Rose "freed us all up as designers" remains Rose's greatest tribute.

Leonard Stanley of Los Angeles, who knew Rose in New York, along with his appreciation of her eye and sense of color, enlightened me about her fondness for wearing hats by Adrian.

Julie Britt, the former wife and good friend of Tom Britt, memorably called Rose "the first hippie" and remembers when she and Tom were Rose's "young friends."

Joanne Creveling opened my eyes to aspects of the relationship between Rose and her sister Dorothy.

I wish to thank Susan Loney, granddaughter of Marjorie Hughes Loney, the half sister of Rose, Eileen, and Dorothy, for her distinctive personal memories.

I am grateful to the many people who helped with the book in ways other than interviews.

Rose's nephew, Anthony Cumming, was tireless, informative, and cheerful in his e-mail memories of Rose, whose favorite nephew he was.

Sarah Cumming Cecil, Rose's great-niece, opened the Cecil family archives, which was of invaluable help.

Oscar de la Renta provided an indelible memory of the appeal of Rose's exotic inventory and the heritage of kindness she embued in her sister Eileen. I also wish to thank Paul O'Regan of Oscar de la Renta, Ltd. for helpfully facilitating Oscar de la Renta's reminiscences.

A longtime friend, David Campbell, an associate of the New York Dessin Fournir showroom, was unfailingly hospitable and summoned up many memories of Eileen Cecil, whom he knew well.

Carl Eric Holmstrom, the partner of the late Ronald Grimaldi, who worked with Eileen Cecil for many years, provided some unique anecdotes about Rose.

Josef Johns, who knew Eileen Cecil and who owns artwork that once graced Rose's house, has been a thorough scholar in providing information about the art and other aspects of Rose's life.

Robert Mahony, professor emeritus of English, Catholic University of America, for rescuing a fragmented 1922 pastel caricature of Rose Cumming and graciously sharing it with us for this project.

Cynthia Cathcart of the Condé Nast Library was hospitable and helpful in facilitating my research among issues of Vogue and *House & Garden* going back to 1917.

Duane Hampton, widow of the late Mark Hampton, provided memories of Rose and was helpful in procuring images of Mark Hampton's wonderful watercolors of Rose's interiors.

I want to thank Paige Rense Noland, editor-in-chief emeritus of *Architectural Digest*, for giving me such a thorough education in the design world over the course of 30 years and for introducing me to many of the people whose memories enliven this book.

At the Dessin Fournir Collections in Plainville, Kansas, I want to thank the following people:

Lora Weigel, who typed the transcripts of my interviews and who said reading them was "like reading a novel."

Scott Gross whose graphic design brought the pages to life.

Jayson K.T. Schwaller who photographed archival documents and paired them with Rose's original interiors.

Kelli Hansen, who drew up contracts and cheered on the progress of the book.

Barb West, who was always cordial in our brief conversations as she passed me on from her switchboard.

And Kim Dague and Jim McGurk who made my visit to Plainville lively, interesting, and comfortable.

She was like Coco Chanel—a self-invented character. She had spotlights on the floor of her dining room with blue gels on them. She was way ahead of her time.

Thomas Britt, interior designer

CHAPTER ONE

"I might become a decorator, but first tell me what that is."

One afternoon in the spring of 1917, right around the time the United States entered World War I, a distinguished older gentleman and a handsome woman, who had the full-bodied silhouette that was still fashionable for women and a face made arresting by dramatic black eyebrows, were lunching in New York's Plaza Hotel. The man was Frank Crowninshield, a bachelor and bon vivant who was known as "the most cultivated, elegant, and endearing man in publishing, if not Manhattan." Crowninshield three years before had been approached by his longtime friend Condé Nast, the magazine publisher, to be the editor of *Vanity Fair*, a new magazine that was supposed to be written by what Dorothy Parker, an early contributor, called "smart alecks" for the smart set. Crowninshield cultivated the era's best writers, such as Parker, Gertrude Stein, T. S. Eliot, and Aldous Huxley. Some of F. Scott Fitzgerald's first stories appeared in *Vanity Fair*, as well as reproductions of paintings by Picasso and Matisse. *Vanity Fair* was the essence of chic. Along with his eye for talent, however, Crowninshield had a shrewd head for business, so that in 1915 *Vanity Fair* contained more pages of advertising than any other magazine in the country.

It was because of Crowninshield's prominent position at the center of the New York world of arts and fashion that the woman, who was Rose Cumming, was lunching with him. She wanted something—most people who approached Crowninshield wanted something—but nevertheless, he was genial and gregarious, and she was ingratiating.

OPPOSITE
Frank Crowninshield, the first editor-in-chief of Vanity Fair, was considered the "most cultivated, elegant and endearing man in publishing, if not Manhattan" in his prime. Here he is on shipboard sometime in the 1920s. *Library of Congress, Bain News Service.*

Rose Cumming, voluptuous, flirtatious and very smart, had a slight English accent, although, in fact, she was Australian. Her introduction to Crowninshield came through her sister, Dorothy Cumming Eliot, a silent film actress, who had come from Australia with an acting troupe a few years earlier. In America, Dorothy had considerable success in silent films, even attracting the notice of the great director, Cecil B. DeMille. Dorothy's sisters, Rose and Eileen, followed her to the United States, where they were later joined by their large mother (she was six feet tall), who aspired to being a grande dame, and their plump little father, who had made money with sheep ranches and in finance.

With a Park Avenue apartment and good looks, it was easy for the Cumming women to launch themselves in society. Rose told people later in life that she had been engaged to a man in England, supposedly her original destination when coming through America, but

after the sinking of the *Lusitania* by the Germans in 1915 the difficulty of travel kept her on this side of the Atlantic. However conveniently imaginary the fiancé may have been, Rose was now settled in New York. Always an opportunist, she arranged the lunch with Frank Crowninshield through Dorothy because, she said, she needed a job. In an exchange that would be the cornerstone for Rose's legendary reputation in the design world, Crowninshield is supposed to have asked, "Perhaps you would like to become a decorator?" And Rose replied, "Perhaps I would, but first tell me what it is."

Decorating—or interior design—was in its infancy in the 1910s, and Rose was not the only person who did not know that making a stylish and comfortable interior could be a business, let alone a profession. Department stores such as A. T. Stewart and Wanamaker's had come of age in the 1860s, after the Crystal Palace Exhibitions of London and New York showed that household goods of all descriptions could be placed together appealingly and generate more business than individual shops. Such grand edifices, chockablock with furniture, china, silver, clothes, and knickknacks, became known as "the palaces of the people," and shopping became a favorite recreation. A practice grew of upholsterers and furniture and fabric salesmen attached to the stores advising customers on choices of colors and how to cram yet more furniture into rooms dizzy with Victorian clutter, but there were no independent decorators.

ABOVE Elsie de Wolfe (1865–1950), a sometime lackluster actress, virtually created the profession of interior design with her new dining room. In 1905, the architect Stanford White commissioned her to design the interiors of the new Colony Club. She is shown here in 1913 in a publicity photograph for her book, *The House in Good Taste*, which was ghost written.
The Granger Collection, New York.

Then, in 1898, Elsie de Wolfe, an unsuccessful actress who cloaked voracious ambition behind a Brooklyn accent and a simpering manner, cleared the bibelots out of the dining room of the little house on New York's Irving Place that she shared with her lover, Elisabeth Marbury, an elephantine theatrical agent, and painted the woodwork white. The world took note and—voilà!—interior design was born.

At about the same time, Edith Wharton, a frustrated wife with impeccable credentials from Old New York Society—who would become one of the great American novelists—published her first book, *The Decoration of Houses*, with architect Ogden Codman. Wharton advocated the same lack of clutter, clean lines, and Neoclassical architectural references that de Wolfe began to show in her interiors. Endorsed by Wharton's social position and authoritative voice, interior design became something to be cultivated by women with Old Money who wanted to do over old houses, and by women with New Money and new houses who wanted social acceptance. "My decorator" became a useful asset for an entrée into society, particularly if the decorator herself (they were all women in the beginning) had or could simulate some social credentials.

ABOVE Ruby Ross Goodnow (1881–1950), also known by the name of her second husband, Chalmers Wood, ghost wrote Elsie de Wolfe's magazine articles and her book. Wood also wrote her own design book, *The Honest House*, and had an illustrious career as a decorator.
Billy Baldwin Collection, courtesy of Adam Lewis.

In 1905, the new Colony Club, founded by a group of young women from old families, erected a clubhouse between Thirty-first and Thirty-second streets on Madison Avenue. It was designed by Stanford White, the most prominent architect in America (who would shortly thereafter be shot on the roof garden of the new Madison Square Garden—one of White's architectural triumphs—by Harry K. Thaw, the insane Pittsburgh steel heir who was White's rival for the favors of the chorine Evelyn Nesbit). As the Colony Club was going up, White asked Elsie de Wolfe to do the interiors. She filled the rooms with clean-lined Louis XVI furniture, painted white, and put treillage, untrimmed trellises, on the walls of the dining room. It was as fresh as paint—de Wolfe was launched.

To further de Wolfe's publicity, a young woman from Georgia named Ruby Ross Goodnow (she would be remembered by her second husband's name as Ruby Ross Wood) was hired to ghostwrite articles about interior design under Elsie de Wolfe's name for a popular women's magazine, *The Delineator*. (The magazine coincidentally was edited by Theodore Dreiser, a further indication of the high literary standard expected in popular journalism at the time.) Goodnow went on to ghostwrite articles for de Wolfe for the *Ladies' Home Journal*,

ABOVE The dining room (c.1895) of the house on Irving
Place shared by Elsie de Wolfe and her partner,
the theatrical agent Elisabeth Marbury. The Victorian
clutter was typical of interiors at the time.
Dining room in the home of Elsie de Wolfe, 1896.
Museum of the City of New York, Byron Co. Collection.

ABOVE The de Wolfe Marbury dining room in 1898.
De Wolfe had begun to shape her career as an interior
decorator, and the world took note of the clean lines
and white paint of the redone dining room.
Dining room in the home of Elsie de Wolfe, 1898.
Museum of the City of New York, Byron Co. Collection.

An elegant dining room created by Rose some time in the 1920s. The painted wallpaper and Chinese screen were characteristic touches.
Collection of the New-York Historical Society, Matte E. Hewitt and Richard A. Smith Collection.

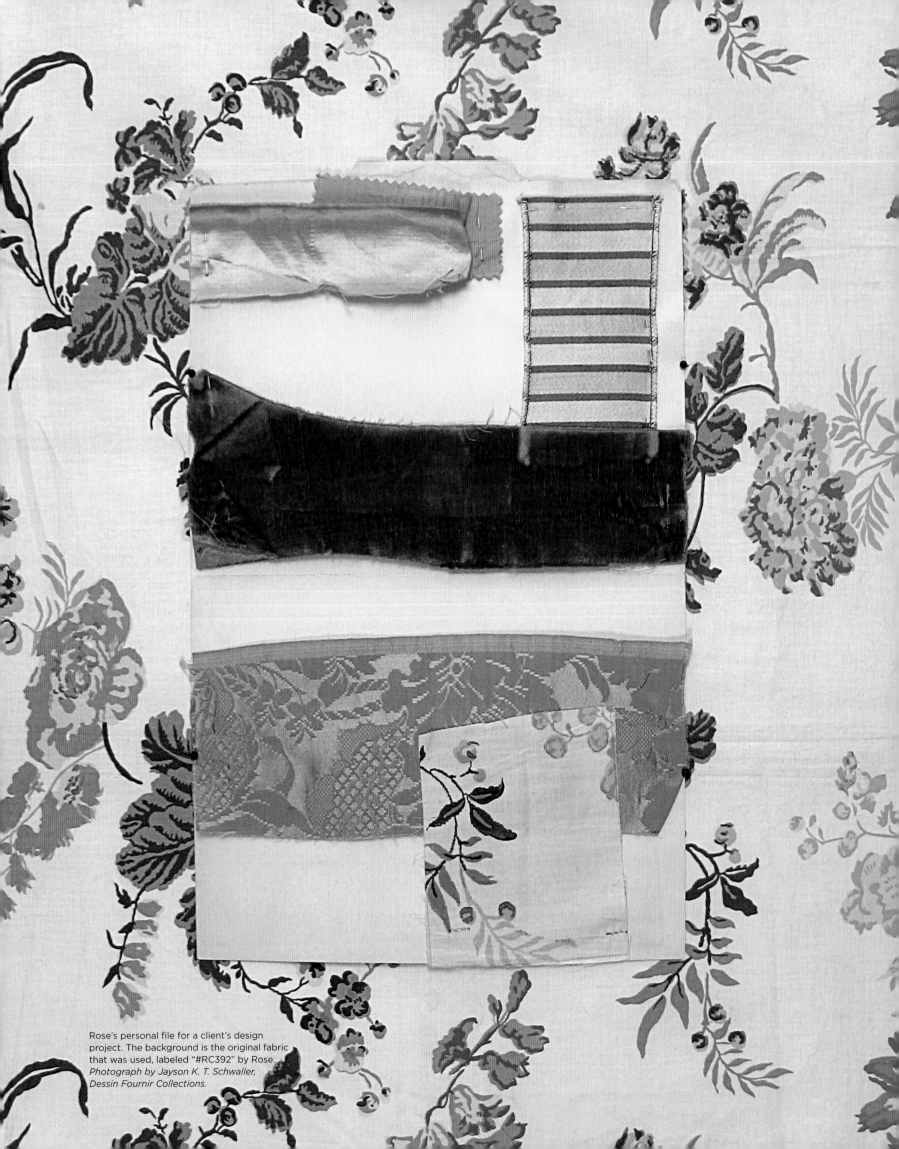

Rose's personal file for a client's design project. The background is the original fabric that was used, labeled "#RC392" by Rose. *Photograph by Jayson K. T. Schwaller, Dessin Fournir Collections.*

A Park Avenue living room decorated by Rose. She was fond of eighteenth-century portraits and shelves to hold such objects as faience cats and milk glass porcelain, both of which she wrote articles about.
Collection of the New-York Historical Society, Matte E. Hewitt and Richard A. Smith Collection.

which were eventually collected and adapted for a decorating manual, *The House in Good Taste*, also published under de Wolfe's name. Some of Goodnow's articles on architecture, which she wrote under her own name for *The Delineator*, came out in book form as *The Honest House* not long afterward.

In the middle 1910s, Goodnow joined the staff of Wanamaker's department store on East Tenth Street and Broadway, across the street from Grace Church, a society temple in every sense of the word. Goodnow ran Belmaison, a decorating department in the store, and worked with Nancy McClelland, who ran Au Quatrième, the store's antiques department. McClelland was a Vassar graduate who had studied art history in Paris, and she also offered decorating services out of Au Quatrième. A scholar with a deep knowledge of the antiques she sold, McClelland also was passionate about historic wallpapers, which she would go on to reproduce in conjunction with the decorating business she founded. As if this was not enough, she also started a home-study course in decorating, sponsored by *Arts & Decoration* magazine.

When Rose Cumming approached Frank Crowninshield for a job suggestion in 1917, Elsie de Wolfe and a society decorator rival of hers named Elsie Cobb Wilson had just gone on the advisory board of the New York School of Fine and Applied Art (now Parsons The New School for Design), which had established the first department of interior decoration in the country. So Frank Crowninshield picked up on what was very much in the air when he suggested that Rose become a decorator. Starting her off, at the age of 30, with the best apprenticeship, "Crownie" sent her to work with a successful society decorator, Mary Buel, known as working ladies were in those days by her husband's name as Mrs. Emmet Buel. Later Rose went to Nancy McClelland at Au Quatrième.

As early as 1918, Rose seemed to be on an antiques buying trip to England, documented by a letter from an Englishwoman thanking her for her "note with Frank Crowninshield's letter of introduction" and promising to be back in London the next week.

Rose's independent streak soon asserted itself, and in 1921, financed by her sister Dorothy's film earnings, Rose opened her own shop offering the art and antiques she had been collecting and furnished with furniture Schmidt Brothers had given her on consignment. Just a few months after opening, however, she came to the shop one morning to find the lock broken and her entire inventory gone. As Rose tells the story:

This was a disaster of the greatest magnitude, and I could not think of a single thing I could do to recover myself. Everything in the world I possessed was gone, and I felt there was no one to whom I could turn for help, as everyone I knew had already helped me. But then along came a messenger, that very day, with a letter. "Friends of yours are distressed to hear of this thing which has befallen you just as you are beginning on your career. We are enclosing a cheque for $5000, and if at any time your loss is less than at the moment [the papers had said it was close to $5000] you can return the difference to the Lincoln Trust Co. on 28th Street." It was for things like this that I grew to love America.

Rose had become a fixture in New York life.

And now it is necessary to go back to the beginnings in the antipodes.

OPPOSITE Rose, looking uncharacteristically sedate, at lunch in the early 1960s with Katharine Tweed, who conceptualized and edited The Finest Rooms, the first book to celebrate interior designers. *Photograph by T. J. Fitzsimmons, Dessin Fournir Collection.*

She was vivacious and wicked.

Albert Hadley, interior designer

CHAPTER TWO

"... just a little girl from Australia ..."

"Rose was just a little girl from Australia," her sister Eileen would say in later years. That suggestion of remote and simple beginnings was true to an extent, but the Australian subcontinent also had all the vigor of a primitive society that was burgeoning with new money and greedy for the experiences and trappings of the Big World. Unlike other British possessions, such as India with its layers of culture that dated back millennia, or even Africa where a thin layer of colonial administration was spread across thousands of miles of open country populated by nomadic tribes, Australia was a frontier society, rather than a colonial one. The indigenous Aborigines were few in number, and they either lived or had been pushed into the inaccessible and arid center of the Australian continent. Australia belonged to the Anglo-Saxon descendents of the British prisoners who had been deported there for the first 75 years of its settlement.

Australians were a brash, muscular people in a new country. Its rich natural resources belonged to them and they were determined to make the most of them. Showy, nouveau-riche displays of luxury coexisted with street brawls and gunfights in the remote "stations" (as the sheep ranches were called), which might be separated by miles in the Outback. A 1905 letter written by a possible suitor to an eighteen-year-old Rose begins, "Thank you so much for your kind letter and the enclosure addressed to Miss Murray Prior. I find that their station is 65 miles from here, but is on my way back to Sydney." Rose had written a letter of introduction, a very proper and usual Victorian way of putting people of "our kind" in touch with each other, for her friend, who had been posted to Brisbane, which she thought was in the neighborhood of another friend, Miss Prior. And, indeed, in Australia 65 miles was not considered much of a separation.

The Cumming girls' mother, Sarah Fennell Hughes Cumming, as a young belle in the 1870s. *Courtesy of Sarah Cumming Cecil.*

The Cumming girls' father, Victor, at the age of twenty-three. He was buoyant, irrepressible, a great gambler and much shorter than his statuesque wife. *Courtesy of Sarah Cumming Cecil.*

The Cumming girls, for all of their quick ways of learning and assumptions of lacquered elegance in later years, were very much a product of the marriage of lingering Victorian formality and the boisterous, rip snorting Down Under. Their mother, who was born Sarah Fennell, was a tall, fulsome beauty. Her first husband, John Hughes, owned a sheep station. The story is that Sarah married him not knowing he was a brute. After she had had a baby with him—a little boy named Jack—he became so abusive and so jealous of her having any social contacts with anyone other than him that she wrapped the baby in a blanket and rode away on horseback in the dark of night. She also had a daughter, Margery, with whom she may have been pregnant when she left John Hughes, who eventually came to America and was a presence in the Cummings' lives.

Sarah's second husband, Victor Cumming, was as safe as houses. A foot shorter than Sarah, plump and cheerful, he was also rich. Rose was born in 1887, Eileen in 1893, and Dorothy in 1895. The girls grew up on a sheep station in a little town called Hurstville, not far from Sydney, where life recalled such American idylls as the Little House series by Laura Ingalls Wilder and *Gone with the Wind*.

The Cumming house in Hurstville, as shown in an early photograph, was a massive mansion built in the Colonial style with a two-story veranda of stone, pierced by heavy Romanesque arches. The verandas marked the house as designed for the tropics, but the weight of the building material eliminated any sense of impermanence. These people were not "going home" to England; they were there to stay—or so it seemed.

In a fragmentary memoir, Rose makes plain her taste early on for adventure, dancing and flirting: As a small child, she was fascinated by the leeches in a nearby pond.

My method of collecting leeches I think shows special ingenuity. I would persuade my baby sister to take a dip in a leech infested pool—beautiful to look at with its willow ringed bank but "definitely out of bounds" for bathing. The method was effective but brutal. After a few minutes Eileen would collect a nice crop of leeches on her soft baby body and I would advance with a bottle and pluck them off at my leisure. Mother, finding the baby mysteriously scarred, laid down the law with a birch rod and thereafter I was forced to do my collecting on my own lip which I found formed excellent bait.

The Cumming family home outside Sydney, Australia. Rose is the little girl under the second arch from the left; Eileen stands at the corner. *Courtesy of Sarah Cumming Cecil.*

Mother and Father[,] like most Australians were both beautiful dancers and were leaders in dancing parties at the neighboring stations where the owners held almost weekly balls. We always stayed overnight at such events. These journeys were a high spot in my life and I remember that rarely was much sleeping done. The youngsters would gather on the stairs to watch the excitement.

My first grown[-]up ball was at the Barry Bay Races. I wore [illegible] and was mortified that my waist was 19 ½ [inches]. Mother has always said that at her first ball her waist was 18 [inches] — but if waists were meant to be small hips were meant to be large and since I weighed only 109 lbs [I] had to make up the deficiency by wearing a hip pad which gave me the required spread.

In the daytime there were races; at night we danced or went on possum hunts where we were all very Edwardian in our determination to take no part in the laughter but to cheer on our respective swains.

The following winter I had my season in Sydney and as all good debutantes do made a bow at Government House parading before the Governor General and making a curtsy in what we imagined was the Buckingham Palace manner. The other great formal balls of the Sydney Season were the Australian Club Ball and the Union Club Ball which were something of a must but the parties we liked best were the informal dances given on the British war ships at least once a week.

A letter to Rose from July 1908, headed the Athenaeum Club, Sydney, from a ship's officer invites her to one of these social events.

Dear Miss Cumming,

Would you and your sisters care to come onboard to tea on Wednesday afternoon[?] A boat leaves [illegible] steps at 3:45. We had a splendid time of it at Jervis Bay — charming spot. We are leaving on Saturday morning for Fiji, so as you may guess this week is passing very quickly with us. Hoping that you will be able to come & would you kindly ask Mrs. Cumming for me if she would also care to come as we would be delighted to see her onboard.

In one's imagination, it is easy to see a version of the Jean Jacques Tissot painting *Ball on Shipboard*, with young ladies in white dresses, hats, and gloves flirting over the cucumber sandwiches with officers in starched white uniforms with knife-sharp creases in their trousers, while stalwart sailors stand at attention in the background. Bunting and sails of many nations hang from the rigging, and the band plays Gilbert and Sullivan and Strauss waltzes. This visual confection is not far from the truth, except that, as Rose would do later in life with social engagements that she hoped might lead to decorating contracts, underneath the raillery, these parties were acts of salesmanship—only here the deadly serious object was marriage. The Cumming girls early on had a taste for adventure and careers, and Victor Cumming had money—he would take solo trips half way around the world every year or two to Monte Carlo to gamble—so there was not the urgency for the Cummings to catch a husband that there was for some young ladies. Nonetheless, it was understood in that time and that place that a good marriage was the only option—socially as well as financially—to give a well-brought-up girl with no acceptable skills independence.

There remains a cluster of invitations, flirtations, and downright love letters written to Rose that are like a bouquet of dried flowers—pale colors and no scent but retaining an aura of their original excitement. An undated letter to "Dear Miss Cumming" says, "I am taking tickets for next Friday for *The Bell of Brittany* & hope this will suit you. Shall be pleased if you will dine at the Australia or Paris House with me." The Australia is the Australian Club, the site of the grandest of Rose's debutante balls. This note has written across the top, "May I bring a friend along?" One presumes this will be a chum to give the host of the evening moral support.

A letter dated October 16, 1911, is both more personal and more tentatively formal. The salutation is also "Dear Miss Cumming." Well into the letter the writer says, "You said on Saturday that occasionally you feel bored in the evenings: do you think you will be feeling bored on Friday week?… The amateur showing *The Importance of Being Earnest* comes off that night, the 27th, and I thought it would be an excellent preventive of boredom, if you would care to use it. I've [tickets] and if you could—and would—come, I would get

another, as I suppose a chaperone would be considered a necessary companion?" After some discussion of his travel plans during the week, he concludes, "Do come if you can—I think you'll enjoy it. I shall have to leave the chaperone question entirely to you!"

The letters become more personal, although still from a number of different men, as time goes on. One dated February 11, 1911, from Gibraltar, Spain, is written on stationery headed "H.M.S. Duke of Edinburgh," with "Fifth Cruiser Squadron, Atlantic Fleet," written by hand below. The salutation on this one is quite a leap from "Dear Miss Cumming" and a discussion of chaperones, because it begins "My dear Fido." The opening is "I wonder…whether you…remember a very rude Midshipman with whom you and Chookie used to be so long-suffering." The midshipman, whose name is Walter Bright-Barton, has seen a photograph of Rose in the cabin of a Captain Scafe on whom he is calling in the Mediterranean, and asked for her address. (A letter to Rose from "your affectionate pal, Robert Charles Scafe," written at about the same time says, "Well, Rose, write to me soon… with a complete catalogue of all the broken hearts.") Bright-Barton is "simply dying" to get back to Australia from Gibraltar, although he thinks that is not likely because Australia "is a very much sought after spot." As interesting evidence of the smoke screen that Rose put up with her flirting, young Bright-Barton asks, "Do write & tell me whether you are engaged yet: I hear that Chookie's time has come—is it true?"

From early 1912, there are two letters from a suitor that reflect Rose's caprice and tactics that verge on cruelty. One way, of course, to keep a beau's interest in those days when a woman had no independent position of her own was to keep him a little off balance. Although Rose's remark that she sometimes was "bored in the evenings" may have been a manipulative angling for a theater invitation, it was also no doubt true that she was frustrated with a stifling provincial life punctuated by parties and gossip and with an uncertain future. In 1912, she was 25—getting on for a debutante. In any case, she put the suitor of January and February 1912—whose name appears to have been Arthur Brooke—through the wringer, although his cringing self-abasement cannot have been particularly attractive.

OPPOSITE Captioned "Freida Hatton's Picnic National Park 1905," this photograph shows Rose (center, wearing the hat with the white trimming) and her friends frolicking. *Courtesy of Sarah Cumming Cecil.*

He begins the letter of January 4, 1912, (after a salutation of "My Dear Rose") complaining of being tired after a journey "mostly from the thought of not seeing you for some time—a most depressing thought" and then continues:

I cannot tell you, dear girl, how much I enjoyed Tuesday evening, in fact Tuesday from 2:30 was just full of joy for me. You often ask me when I like you best—well that day was one of your best; there was a je ne sais quoi [oh, come on, Arthur, surely you can do better than that], just something about you that if possible was sweeter than usual—& I hated leaving you. You were quite right when you said I could not bear you out of my sight, for when you are I am just always thinking about you. I go to sleep thinking of you and wake up with the same thought. You also said your letters could only be about what you had been doing—Why, Why can't you let me have a few of your thoughts also—not the sort you gave me on the telephone though—when you said in a most frigid tone of voice that you would not see me anymore—that you had had enough of me. I wonder very much what made you say it. I have a horrid feeling sometimes, that you really meant it, & especially after this last week when I have been so stupid & uninteresting, but be a dear and make some allowances because I have been a bit off colour… I wonder what sort of a time you had at the theater last night, not too ecstatic I hope—I am a selfish beast—I hate to think of you having too grand a time with other people.

The photograph is a great joy & helps to keep off the "blues," but be sweet and write me a nice letter full of thoughts just to dispel some of the gloom I am suffering from. Take care of yourself & don't work yourself to death in the way you usually do.

Yours devotedly,

Arthur

In February, Rose has Arthur squirming again—and in a major way:

Dearest Girl,
How I annoyed and irritated you yesterday I am unable to tell, but something happened which I am quite unable to account for. I have thought a good deal about you since I saw you last night, and am feeling pretty wretched. One or two things you said yesterday were not quite kind, and hurt a good deal, probably more because I am very fond of you, Rose, although you do not think so, and I suppose

this makes one more sensitive than one would be otherwise. It was not like you, dear girl [!], and I cannot believe you meant to be unkind. Do be a dear sweet child and not a cross peevish one, and write and tell me I was mistaken. I left rather abruptly last night, but I felt you were out of sympathy with me and would only make things worse by staying also I confess to feeling just a bit sore.

Do send me a line as soon as you decide the day you are leaving….

Au revoir[,] dear Rose.

Always yours devotedly,

Brooke

Arthur seems to have erased himself from the picture, perhaps from all the self-deprecation, but other suitors surged to the fore. One, who only signed himself "Samuel," wrote a long vivid account of traveling "upcountry" in New Zealand. The letter is very entertaining—and worth quoting at some length—but it also gives an idea of the brooding countryside in both colonies, Australia and New Zealand, that lay just beyond the few cities. There was a cluster of activity in the harbors commercially—and socially on British Navy ships for a young woman of Rose's social background—but just out of sight of city lights, there was the bush.

Samuel's letter is headed Wellington, New Zealand, the year after Arthur's correspondence, and it begins with the usual uncertainty about Rose's mood:

My dearest Rose,

It was with great delight I discovered a letter from you this morning amongst my little pile. Rather a nice one too, as I quite expected a rowing which no doubt I deserved.

He then gets into his expedition:

Well since I wrote you last I have experienced a little of the rough side of Colonial life. It started with a 50-mile coach drive over the mountains raining cats & dogs & bitterly cold with snow all round. Not expecting this kind of weather I was attired in a thin flannel suit & no underclothes to speak of. That I am still alive & well is surprising. I was the only passenger in this vehicle they call a coach. One does not quite expect the same turnouts as one sees at a meet of the four-in-hand club but one has a right to expect something in the way of springs & cushions of some sort on the seat. The boards of the floor were mostly missing & the wind blew up my trousers. However I eventually arrived at Tokaanu very much bruised and battered — chilled to the marrow and out of temper. A hot bath out of doors in a natural hot spring coupled with a hot drink did much to improve matters. After something they called dinner I was conducted to my room which was a wooden edifice at the other end of the village. The whole affair was the room & the room was the whole affair. I mean there were no other rooms. I was left here with a candle & a stretcher bed — no furniture, carpet or anything in the way of luxuries, just bare, very bare, necessities. There were a few potatoes in one corner of the room which were unnecessary otherwise everything there was essential.

Next morning I & my bunk etc. were rowed out to the fishing camp [the reason for his expedition]. This consisted of two or three tents & a wooden shed. However the tents appeared cleaner than my previous night's quarters so I felt more or less satisfied. I went out in a boat & caught a fish or two — fine fellows they were. After dinner & a chat with a parson who was the only mate I had at the camp I retired to my tent for sleep. Various sorts of animals [and] birds[,] etc[.,] seemed to be prowling around outside the tent & all sorts of strange noises I listened to. Rats were my worst trouble. They ran about all round the tent inside without ceremony or fear & my bed being very low to the ground they would sometimes jump on it & run about till I frightened them off, which was not long if I was awake.

We had a cook & bottle washer who was a cheery soul[,] but everything was badly cooked & dirty. The first night I complained that my tea spoon was greasy & consequently grease was floating on my tea. Our cook resented my complaint & told me to remember I was in camp. However he took the spoon, rubbed it in his filthy apron, breathed on it & flung it back at me.

Samuel does some more fishing, which he seems to enjoy, says what towns he is going to next in New Zealand, when he comes down out of the mountains, and then concludes,

[N]ot one woman have I seen who is not positively ugly. Perhaps having been basking in the sunlight of the exceedingly beautiful recently has spoilt my appetite.

Well au revoir Rosie dear, think of me sometimes & don't flirt too hard with "juicy boy."

Late in life Rose's sister Eileen said about their youth in Australia and the reason for their subsequent coming to America, "We felt so bottled up." There was little to do in Australia for girls of their class except to flirt and hope it would lead to marriage, and this exchange of letters suggest Rose at least made a show of playing the game. But in 1912, Rose took steps to change this situation, although at first it was a trial lateral move. She had a beau whom she had presumably met in Australia, who was a tea planter in Ceylon. Rose went to Ceylon.

Leonard Woolf, the writer, publisher, and husband of the famous novelist Virginia Woolf, had been a civil servant in Ceylon in the imperial British administration (Ceylon was a British colony) between 1907 and 1911. His biographer, Victoria Glendinning, describes the colony:

Ceylon, renamed Sri Lanka in 1972, was where Sinbad the Sailor was washed up in The Thousand and One Nights. *Arab mariners called it Serendib, from which the word "serendipity" was coined. It is like a teardrop falling from the southern tip of India, and about the same size as Ireland or Tasmania. Over more than a millennium, an evolved artistic and technological culture was supported by an irrigation system of huge reservoirs — 'tanks' — many of which survive in use.*

The people were a mix of native Sinhalese, Hindus from the Indian mainland, and descendents of Portuguese and Dutch colonists who had intermarried with the Sinhalese and Hindus. The island had been under British rule since the late eighteenth century, and the British colonial administrators, army and naval officers, and commercial people kept themselves strictly separate from—and, as they thought, above—the permanent inhabitants. Victoria Glendinning speaks to the situation of people like Rose:

Young British women, when in the towns, flirted with civil servants and naval and army officers and were dangled in front of suitable ones by their elders. Marriage was the only way forward, and marrying a 'native' was not an acceptable option.

This would have all been very like Australia for Rose, except that for a backdrop to the flirting, instead of the lower classes speaking with guttural Cockney accents in a desolate Outback, there was the rich tapestry of the jungle, ancient ruined cities, beautiful silks in jewel tones, exotic inhabitants, and richly colored animals and birds. Along with Rose's dictum later in life that "parrots are blue and green, why shouldn't fabrics be," her bold unorthodox sense of color, her taste for bizarre furniture, and even the famous "ugly room" in her house with its prints and carvings of predatory animals may have come from imbibing the rich atmosphere of Ceylon. Although Rose learned a great deal about European antiques after she got to New York, her taste was completely her own and there was always a hint of Eastern magic about it. The world-famous decorator Mario Buatta, known as "The Prince of Chintz," knew Rose when he was young and today he says simply, "She created fantasy." It is likely that she first found the elements of that fantasy in Ceylon.

As to the beau, Gilbert, himself, he seems to have been much like the others, completely enraptured by Rose. Whoever said "love makes you stupid" could have been describing Rose's suitors with their strangled prose and repeated protestations of devotion (the exception is Samuel with his graphic and funny description of the fishing camp in New Zealand).

Gilbert's letters are written on the letterhead of the Galle Face Hotel in Colombo, which is where he apparently was staying in the capital while down from his tea platation. Gilbert's first letter (they corresponded even though it appears they were staying in the same hotel) says,

Rose[,] I am enclosing you a photo of a fellow who is madly in love with you and would give his soul for you if only you would marry him.

He continues significantly,

Rose you want to have a good time when you get married so you will and if I should happen to be the lucky man you shall have everything that you want and it would be my intention to take you to live in England where you could have a much better time.

Gilbert's relationship with Rose goes along the predictable route of self-pity:

Dearest Rose, What about tonight as I see your Australian friends are still here? I am going up country first thing in the morning and I only hope you will spend this last evening with me. Rose[,] I have been all by myself this afternoon and had a pretty thin time.

Then expensive gifts coupled with self-pity:

Dearest will you either give my boy [that is, my servant] my signet ring with the crest on it or bring it down with you, the other one is a bargain which we made this afternoon. I do so wish you were not going away tomorrow as I don't know what on earth I am ever going to do without you and as you know or I hope you do that you are everything in the world to me now. It really seems so unkind that you should have to go away tomorrow and leave me to it. I think I shall go and bury myself on the estate and never see another person.

Gilbert soon pops the question and Rose refuses him. He goes to pieces in a particularly Victorian and obsequious way:

My darling Rose,

I am writing to say that I am very sorry for being such a beast to you. Rose[,] I was and am still very much in love with you and as you will fully understand when I got your reply tonight it rather knocked all the stuffing out of me[;] however you have made up your mind as you told me before dinner and now we are nothing but great pals. As far as I can see Rose there is only one thing in my favour and that is that I have never attempted to take any liberties with you such as try to kiss you and[,] love[,] I think you may possibly consider this to be one point in my favour[,] although if you only knew what I had gone through refraining from this you would perhaps understand my affection towards you a little more. Rose may I as a great pal[,] and also to show that you like me if only a little[,] kiss you[?] I will not try to do so until I have your permission.

Had he kissed her without permission, she might have married him.

Later that night Gilbert writes another letter with more apologies, saying Rose may keep the ring. This letter is addressed on the corner of the outside: "Miss R.S. Cumming, Room No. 15."

OPPOSITE AND ABOVE A letter from Gilbert, the English tea planter in Ceylon whom Rose went to see, both of them staying in separate rooms in the hotel. Gilbert in abject tones asks Rose for his signet ring back, but says that the "other ring is a bargain which we made this afternoon." Gilbert's obsequious misery is typical of the state to which Rose reduced her suitors. *Courtesy of Sarah Cumming Cecil.*

47

My dearest Rose,

Just a few lines to say how very sorry I am about tonight and I only hope you will forgive me. I am also very sorry for breaking down in the way in which I did[,] but something broke and so perhaps you will now fully understand the reason for it. Rose I only hope you know how much I really love you as you are the only treasure in the world that I ever wanted[;] but I have your friendship and this will make up for a very great deal…The little present which you received today I hope you will always wear and think of the man who was and is still very much in love with you and will do anything in his power for you however big or small it may be.

Gilbert's letters continue with more energy when he is back on his tea plantation and describing his work and the natural disasters with which he contends. In a letter of December 21, 1912, he says, "I have lots of work to attend to what with the manufacture of rubber, etc." In addition to the growing of tea, coffee, cinnamon, sugar, and indigo, Ceylon was beginning to harvest and export rubber, particularly necessary for the newly ubiquitous automobile tires. In fact, in a January 2, 1913, letter Gilbert commends Rose for taking an automobile ride while she is visiting "up country."

I am so glad you enjoyed your motor drive on Sunday and I think it is by far the best way of seeing the country…Well now you have been on an estate what do you think of it and how do you think you would like the life[? Y]ou would now know how to make tea quite well[;] don't you think it is very interesting? How do you like Kandy [the old Sinhalese capital in the center of the country? D]on't you think it is very pretty all along the lake[;] I quite agree with you that the cinnamon gardens are very pretty.

After another letter later in the month, when Rose is on shipboard, presumably returning to Australia, a letter describing a cataclysmic flash flood on his plantation, but also filled with the usual imprecations against flirting ("I am simply longing…to hear what sort of voyage you are having and also how many men have fallen in love with you and proposed but perhaps the ring has been something to guard them against!"), Gilbert fades away into the jungle.

During the years that Rose was flirting and dancing in the jungle of the colonial marriage market, the fledgling interior decoration profession was getting a toehold in New York. The famed Paris correspondent for *The New Yorker*, Janet Flanner, writing a profile of Elsie de Wolfe in January of 1938, said, "Twenty years after [one of de Wolfe's best roles as an actress in 1895] she had made a million and an international name by inventing the new fashionable profession of interior decorating." One substantial endorsement of de Wolfe's work, in addition to Stanford White's Colony Club, which he had commissioned her to decorate in 1905, was the assignment to furnish and decorate the private quarters on the second floor of Henry Clay Frick's Neoclassical mansion built between 1913 and 1914 on Fifth Avenue at Seventieth Street. Frick paid de Wolfe a ten percent commission on all the furniture she bought for the rooms, and there were millions and millions of dollars worth of it. The formal public rooms downstairs now house The Frick Collection.

De Wolfe's book (ghostwritten by Ruby Ross Goodnow Wood), *The House in Good Taste*, came out in 1913, followed by Goodnow's own book, *The Honest House*, in 1914. Building on Edith Wharton and Ogden Codman's *The Decoration of Houses* (1898), these books codified the profession. There were also newly hatched professional academic training programs for would-be interior decorators. The New York School of Fine and Applied Arts had included a department of interior decoration in their curriculum since 1907, taught by Frank Alvah Parsons, whose name would one day grace the school. In 1916, a man named Sherrill Whiton began offering a mail order "Home Study Course in the Decorative Arts," which led to the formation some years later of the New York School of Interior Decoration, now the New York School of Interior Design. Ruby Ross Wood and Nancy McClelland joined the advisory board there.

Frank Parsons' own 1915 textbook, *Interior Decoration: Its Principles and Practice*, emphasized color, form, balance, scale, and texture as the guiding principles of interior decoration, and particulars of Wharton, de Wolfe, and Goodnow-Wood's credos would be prominent elements of Rose Cumming's design philosophy. Wharton and Codman, as well as the academic programs, advocated the use of genuine antiques, preferably French, and eighteenth-century styles of furniture as opposed to the wild experimentation in reproduction styles that had been favored by the Victorians, which the invention of the jigsaw and other technology had permitted. Goodnow-Wood wrote in *The Honest House*:

The work of the colonial builders has been replaced by the crude effort of the recent contractor. The fine old farmhouses of two generations ago have been replaced by idiotic colored turrets and rotundas…Our small houses for a long time have been growing more complex; simple roof lines have been replaced by forms resembling the clocks of the Black Forest [cuckoo clocks]…We have substituted in our endeavor to improve upon the old forms, an endless number of superficial and unnecessary elements in the main of exceedingly bad taste, such as is illustrated in the product of the jigsaw and the turning lathe.

As well as advocating simplicity like her peers, some of Elsie de Wolfe's particular tastes forecast similar ones in Rose. De Wolfe liked chintz (hitherto thought of as only appropriate for country cottages) and pale woodwork; she liked French antiques, which she mixed with painted and stenciled furniture; she abhorred all the furniture in a room "matching"; and, most amazingly of all—forecasting Rose's comment about the colors of parrots—de Wolfe liked to combine greens, purples, and lavenders. Her credo was: "You will express yourself in your house whether you want to or not, so it had better be good."

Goodnow had opened a design company called The Modernist Studios in 1914, the year her book came out. The designs she promoted in her studios were inspired by the Wiener Werkstätte, the cutting-edge cooperative of artists, textile and ceramic designers, furniture designers, architects, and craftspeople that had been founded in Vienna more than ten years before. New York was not ready for such avant-garde designs with their hard edges, lack of ornament, and bold colors and Goodnow's studios failed. The fact that she had made the attempt was noteworthy, however, and retreating only a bit into a more traditional aesthetic, she joined Wana-

maker's department store to work with Nancy McClelland in her antiques and interiors department.

Design as a profession was launched and proving seaworthy, but before Rose got on board she had to travel halfway around the world away from a storm that would pull the world as she had known it apart.

On July 28, 1914, Austria declared war on Serbia. World War I had begun.

She loved adventure and she wasn't afraid of anything.

Anthony Cumming,
aviator and Rose Cumming's nephew

CHAPTER THREE

A Sea Change

World War I was the costliest war in terms of human life that has ever been fought. Seventy million combatants were engaged, making it the largest war in history; 15 million soldiers were killed.

Australia, far from the theater of conflict, was nonetheless an enthusiastic part of the British Empire and young men rushed to enlist. From a population of fewer than five million people, 416,809 men enlisted, over 60,000 of who were killed, and 156,000 were wounded, gassed, or taken prisoner before the war was over. Most Australian recruits accepted into the army in August 1914 were sent to Egypt, rather than Europe, to fight the Ottoman Empire, which had entered the conflict on the side of the Central Powers.

Rose and her family received their customary number of letters from young men in the army. One, from around Christmas 1915, has a salutation to "Dearest Auntie," presumably the Cumming girls' mother, and it is signed "your loving nephew, Charles." There is virtually nothing about the war in this letter, perhaps because Charles was ordered into "hospital" in Egypt with dysentery on his way to the trenches in France, the trenches where the Allies and the Germans faced each other in deadly stalemate for much of the war. "I will write another long letter, describing the trenches, as I expect to be there by the time you get this," Charles writes optimistically.

We do not know whether Charles survived the trenches (or even dysentery), but he goes on at some length about the sights he saw before dysentery felled him. "Cairo, I think, is about the dirtiest city in the world. It is full of disease, & absolutely stinks. I have only been there twice & that was quite enough. I spend my time in Heliopolis, which

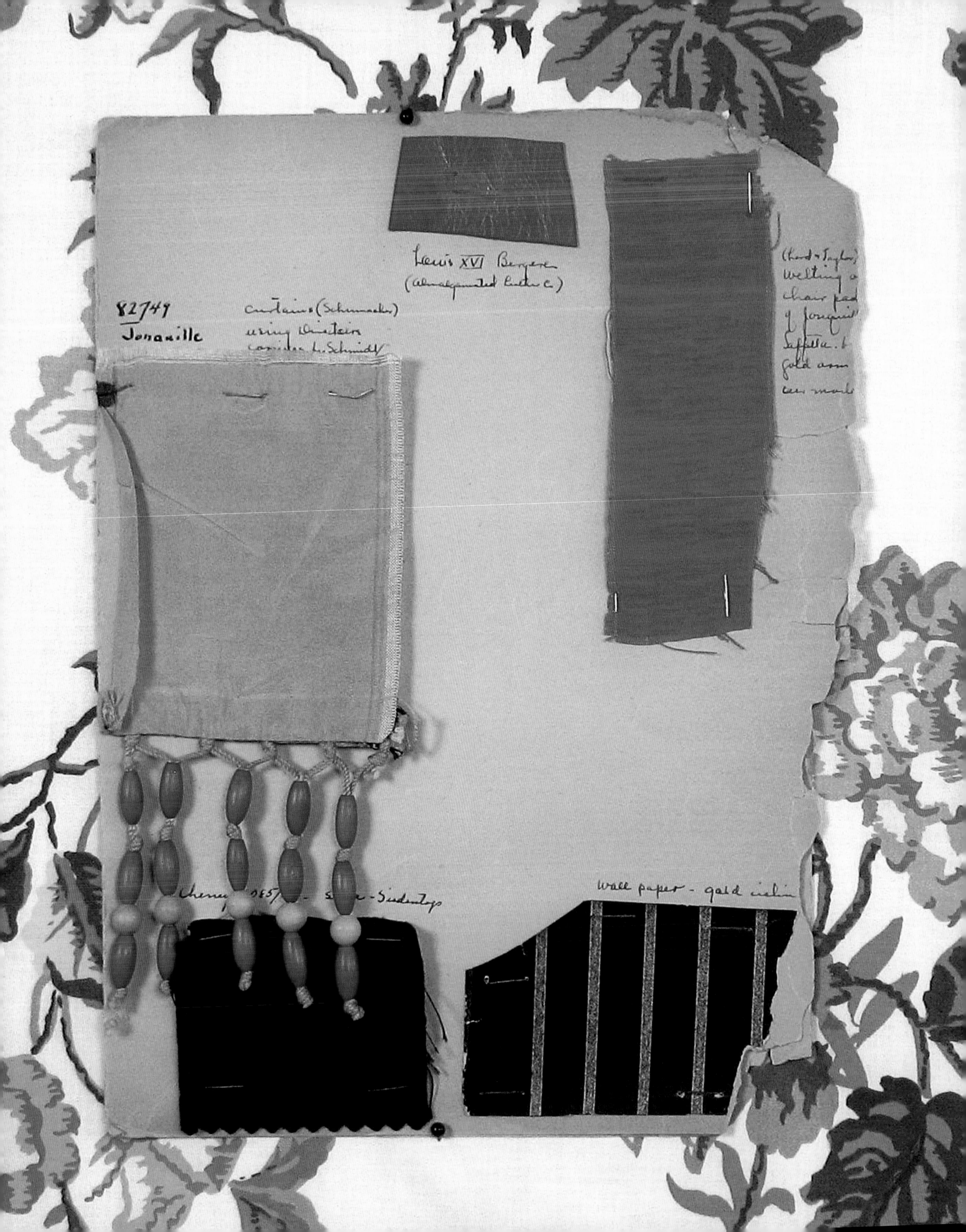

Louis XVI Bergere
82749
curtains (Schumacher)
Welting
chair pad
gold
Wall paper - gold

A page from Rose's design files for a client set against "Eileen," one of her original shop fabrics still in the collection today.
Photograph by Jayson K . T. Schwaller, Dessin Fournir Collections.

is a model suburb. Beautiful buildings, French, Greek, Spanish & Italian girls & Australian nurses in droves." Charles thinks the Cairo zoo "knocks the Sydney [zoo] into a cocked hat"; the museum is full of "old relics;" and the pyramids are "very interesting…We climbed the highest of them. It is 470 feet high & that many square at the base. From the top you have a good view of the R. Nile, (which at the time was in flood & as far as you could see, there were houses half submerged)."

A letter to Rose, dated December 21, 1915, is signed "your affectionate cousin Cec." The head of the letter is the YMCA logo with the motto "For God, For King & For Country" above it, and the subhead "The Mediterranean Expeditionary Force" below. "Cec"—or Cecil one assumes—is in a rest home in Egypt, but apparently far sicker than Charles. He had an operation in September for a cyst on his spine; the procedure was botched and had to be repeated. Cecil says, "I am very weak and my nerves are almost completely gone."

His debilitation does not keep Cecil from wanting to recover, however, because "I am looking forward to having a go at 'Jacko,' which is the name the Australians have given the Turks." The Australian and New Zealand forces (known by the acronym ANZAC for "Australian and New Zealand Army Corps") landed on the Gallipoli Peninsula on April 25, 1915. From this position, they were to hold the steep slopes above the beach and break through the Turkish lines at the top, according to a plan to ultimately capture Istanbul that had been developed by Winston Churchill, then First Lord of the Admiralty. The Turks, under the leadership of Kemal Ataturk, who would create the modern nation of Turkey after the war, tried to drive the Australians off the peninsula, but a stalemate ensued until December. Cecil makes scathing remarks about the British officers and soldiers he has seen from his rest home in Alexandria:

[They] are of a very poor quality. If you saw them you would not have too much confidence of beating the Germans…Most of them are mere kids, and have no heart whatever [for fighting], as has been proved on the [Gallipoli] Peninsula, when our chaps [the Australians] carried a position in a good many instances the Tommies

LEFT Although this is only an anteroom on East Fifty-fifth Street, it shows all of Rose's attention to detail in the wall murals and the satin upholstery.
Collection of the New-York Historical Society, Matte E. Hewitt and Richard A. Smith Collection.

57

[the nickname for British soldiers] were put in to hold it, but left it to Jacko, and our boys had to retake same and hold it…Our chaps have so far easily proved themselves the best fighters on the Peninsula, which is going to be an absolute failure to all appearances.

Indeed, Cecil was right. After eight months of a standoff between the British and Australians on one side and the Turks on the other, the British and Australians evacuated the peninsula on December 19th and 20th under cover of a comprehensive, deceptive operation that fooled the Turks, who thus inflicted very few casualties at that point. The evacuation was the most successful part of the Gallipoli Peninsula campaign, in which more than 8,000 Australian and 1,200 New Zealand soldiers died over the eight months of the siege. April 25, the date of the landing on the Gallipoli Peninsula, is a national holiday to this day known as ANZAC Day in honor of the soldiers' sacrifices in both Australia and New Zealand. It was a day honored in New York by Rose and her sister Eileen all their lives.

A third letter from a soldier named Roy tells Rose that "I had the luck to belong to the last party to leave the ANZAC trenches [on the Gallipoli Peninsula] at 2:10 AM on the morning of 20th Dec, and have the satisfaction of having gone through from the landing to the evacuation, and am the only officer of the battalion who has done so." Roy's battalion was sent to Alexandria, where he says he saw Cecil.

With the western world in disruption, the Cumming sisters felt more than ever as though they were in a backwater in Australia where only the imagined sound of distant gunfire kept them alert to what was going on at the center of events. To their great credit, considering their sheltered and privileged colonial upbringing, all three Cumming girls were eager to build careers, rather than simply marry well.

Dorothy, the youngest, was the first to fly the coop, and she did it in a way that was quite literally dramatic. Dorothy ran away and joined, not the circus, but what was almost equally shocking for a well-brought-up young lady, the theater. J.C. Williamson Ltd. was the largest and best known theater company in Australia and, in fact, in the first decades of the twentieth century, it was the largest theater company in the world, employing 650 people. Dorothy Cumming (who told

RIGHT A page from Rose's design files for a client including a note calling for "glass curtains." The fabric is an original hand-block print called "Grand Fleur." *Photograph by Jayson K. T. Schwaller, Dessin Fournir Collections.*

people for most of her life that she had been born in 1899 when in fact she was born in 1895) was barely 17 when she joined Williamson's troupe around 1912. With beauty, some talent, and the drive of a locomotive, she quickly made her mark, garnering lead roles and playing opposite such theater luminaries as the legendary Cyril Maude in his signature comedy, *Grumpy*, and *Sheridan's School for Scandal*.

J. C. Williamson had a subsidiary film company, as well as a theater company, and Dorothy made her film debut in 1915. (She would go on to make 39 films in Australia and America.) Released in America as *Within Our Gates*, the Australian title for the film was *Deeds That Won Gallipoli*. Films were made in a matter of weeks, or at the most a couple of months then; and that optimistic title showed that even before the fight for the Gallipoli Peninsula was resolved, which did not happen until the evacuation of the Australian troops in December of 1915, the battle for Gallipoli had become iconic in the Australian imagination.

Dorothy went to Canada, probably with Williamson, which had theaters throughout the British Dominions, no later than 1915, and from there she went to New York, where the movie industry was then based. The first of her films made in the United States was *Snow White*, released in 1916. *Snow White* was made by the Famous Players-Lasky Corporation; it was produced by Adolph Zukor and Daniel Frohman. Zukor, who was one of the greatest of the early film moguls, ultimately creating Paramount Pictures, had merged his Famous Players Film Company with the Jesse L. Lasky Feature Play Company only in 1916, the year of *Snow White*. In the film Dorothy was cast as Queen Brangomar, the wicked queen who is the bane of the innocent Snow White, thus beginning a career of playing icy, often malign, albeit beautiful women. The American movie industry for its first ten or 12 years was centered in studios in Astoria, Queens. Although it is true that, beginning in 1910, D. W. Griffith, who created the modern cinema, took his Biograph Company to a little country village named Hollywood in Southern California for half the year, because the weather offered such wonderful conditions

LEFT A couch entirely upholstered in satin jewel tones would reappear in Rose's library on Fifty-third Street. Here it was done for a client on East Fifty-fifth Street. *Collection of the New-York Historical Society, Matte E. Hewitt and Richard A. Smith Collection.*

61

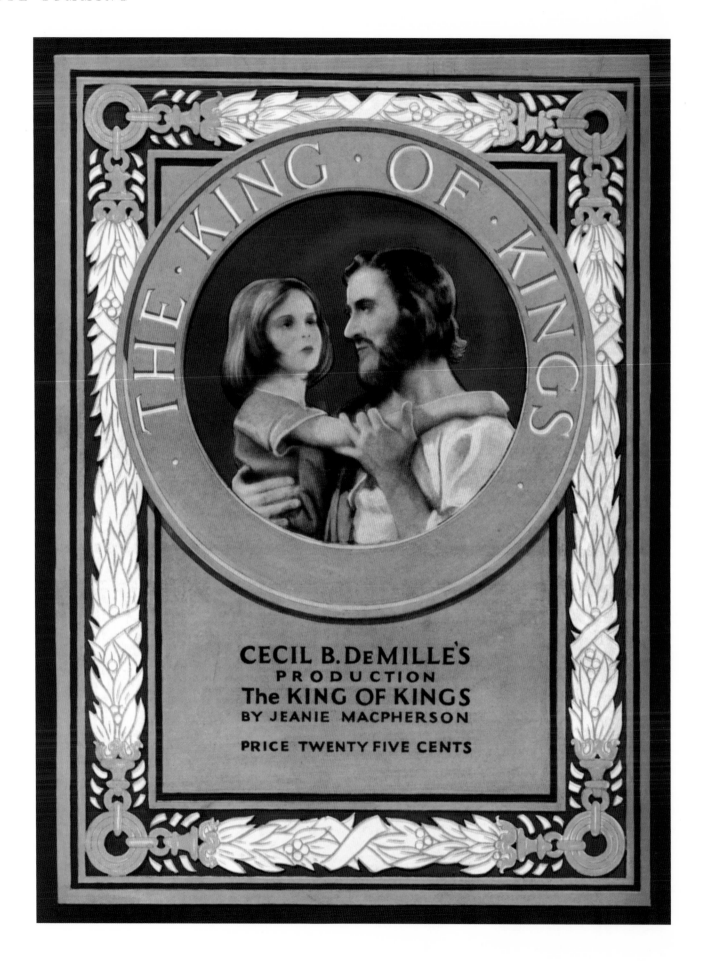

for filming, the industry was not based there until late in the decade. In 1916, Famous Players-Lasky Corporation had studios at Sixth Avenue and Pierce Avenue in Long Island City. Dorothy would have had access to ("been exposed to" is too passive a description for a woman of her ambition) the New York theater world. This no doubt led to her starring in *Tiger! Tiger!*, a successful play by Edward Knoblock, on Broadway in 1918, one of her few stage roles after she entered the movies.

Sometime, almost certainly in 1916, Dorothy, having hit the social and even financial jackpot—with glamour thrown in—cabled Australia to summon Rose and Eileen to New York. There is a letter to Rose from London, dated September 9, 1917, from Arthur Brooke, the self-abasing suitor of five years before in Australia ("I have been so stupid and uninteresting…"), that says, "I have always been expecting to get across to New York for some time past…," so we know that Rose was in New York by 1917.

Arthur's letter is interesting in several ways. He seems to have acquired some gumption with success and a very good British address. He says, "I am living a funny sort of life at present—half the week here [?] and half the week in London. I have rather a nice flat in Piccadilly overlooking the Green Park—come over soon and see it." Arthur's injunction somewhat puts the lie to Rose's long polished story that she was on her way to England to be married when she was marooned in New York by an embargo on women sailing across the Atlantic. This is particularly so because Arthur's next paragraph begins, "You surely will come across before the war is over. I do so want to be able to show you a little of London."

It is very likely that the fictive impossibility of travel, along with the straw figure of Arthur in the distance, was convenient for an unmarried Rose in later years to hold up as the reason for her spinsterhood. Although Arthur says in his letter, "I would love to see you again, and see if I could spoil you as you say. It would be quite like old times," he does not seem to be too serious about it. The letter continues, "things seem to have changed so during the last few years & I sometimes wonder if I am getting really old." He ends

affectionately but coolly, "I hope Rose in spite of my long silence that you still have a kind spot in your heart for me, yours very sincerely, Brooke."

In a postscript Arthur writes, "I scan the *Melbourne Punch* each week for news of Dorothy." Dorothy was now international news and right next to her in New York was exactly where Rose wanted to be. To ensure that she stayed there, she had lunch with Mr. Crowninshield.

Frank Crowninshield, as we have said, was editor in chief of *Vanity Fair* and at the epicenter of the worlds of style and art in New York. Vanity Fair was not only smart, it was intelligent. *Vanity Fair* opened New York—and stylish America—to the arts.

One of Frank Crowninshield's closest friends was Otto Kahn, an international financier and patron of the arts, who will come into our story in a major way a little later. Kahn wrote that *Vanity Fair* was "engaging, bright, interesting, spiritual, discriminating…undeviating in its adherence to the canons of good taste, gay, good-looking and stylish, with a serious purpose behind its dashing ways." Through her association with Crowninshield, Rose would have access to this world. As evidence of *Vanity Fair*'s light touch on serious matters, the cover of the April 1917 issue—the month of Rose and Frank Crowninshield's lunch and also the date of the United States entering World War I—has a drawing of two young female chorines wearing army uniforms and saluting in a synchronized dance before a chattering nightclub audience.

The stylish New York that Rose was introduced to in 1917 was about to change dramatically over the next decade. Just as her travels from Australia covered an enormous distance and she was exposed to a kind of urban sophistication that had its own considerable distance from the provincial society in which she had been a belle, so would Rose and the western world go through yet another sea change between 1917 and 1930.

OPPOSITE The culmination of Rose's sister Dorothy's career as a silent film star was playing the Virgin Mary in Cecil B. deMille's *King of Kings* in 1926. *Courtesy of Sarah Cumming Cecil.*

Only Yesterday, an entertaining and informative social history written by journalist Frederick Lewis Allen in 1931, details the changes America went through in the decade of the 1920s. The book sets the scene of the old, pre-1920s world with a "Prelude: May, 1919." A fictional, upper-middle-class young couple, "Mr. and Mrs. Smith," come down to breakfast:

From the appearance of Mr. Smith as he comes to the breakfast table on this May morning of 1919, you would hardly know that you are not in the nineteen-thirties. The movement of men's fashions is glacial. It is different, however, with Mrs. Smith. She comes to breakfast in a suit, the skirt of which — rather tight at the ankles — hangs just six inches from the ground. She has read in Vogue *the alarming news that skirts may become even shorter…but six inches is still the orthodox clearance. Mrs. Smith may use powder, but she probably draws the line at paint. Although the use of cosmetics is no longer, in 1919, considered* prima facie *evidence of a scarlet career, and sophisticated young girls have already begun to apply them with some bravado, most well-brought-up women still frown upon rouge … [and] Mrs. Smith has never heard of such dark arts as that of face-lifting. Mr. and Mrs. Smith discuss a burning subject, the High Cost of Living…Mrs. Smith, confronted with an appeal from Mr. Smith for economy, reminds him that milk has jumped since 1914 from nine to fifteen cents a quart, sirloin steak from twenty-seven to forty-two cents a pound, butter from thirty-two to sixty-one cents a pound, and fresh eggs from thirty-four to sixty-two cents a dozen. [Rose, living on Park Avenue, was probably not too concerned about the price of eggs — and in any case she showed an aristocratic disregard for money all her life — but the comparisons are interesting.]…Mr. and Mrs. Smith have been invited to a tea dance at one of the local hotels…If the hotel is up to the latest wrinkles, it has a jazz-band instead of the traditional orchestra for dancing.*

ABOVE
Otto Kahn (1867–1934) was an international financier and railroad magnate. Supporter of the arts and movies, he was a friend of Dorothy's and may have been Rose's lover and financial backer.
The Granger Collection, New York.

The *New York Times* has advertisements for eight different jazz bands between February and April of 1917. One is the Original Dixieland Jazz Band, which played at Reisenweber's in Columbus Circle; and another is the New Orleans Jazz Band, which was a group of white musicians with Jimmie Durante as the front man and pianist, which played at Rector's on Broadway at Forty-eighth Street, where there was entertainment on "both floors."

To continue briefly with the Smiths: "[At the tea dance] there is one French officer in blue…a foreign uniform adds the zest of war-time romance to any party." Finally, the writer mentions that after dinner the Smiths may go to the theater to see such a popular play as *Tiger! Tiger!*—the one Broadway hit in which Dorothy Cumming made her appearance.

Apropos of the French officer in blue, Rose, who was nothing if not up to the minute, had two European beaux—one Russian and one French—who wrote her the most touching letters in her collection over a number of years. The Russian, who is known only by his initials N. P., wrote from Seattle, where he had gone from New York in preparation for going to Tokyo and then on to Vladivostock.

My darling Rose,
I send you from my last stop in America my love. I miss you so much, think only I am now five days without your dear care, not seeing your sweet eyes and hearing your voice. How I hate that on account of my poor English I am not able to write you a long and nice letter, to tell you what I just would like. Anyhow, be sure darling, I will never forget you, all my life long I will always love those happy hours we spent together and think with gratitude and admiration of you. Your dear image will not be forgotten by your big boy. Don't forget to write me[.] […]accurately remember I am now a homeless countryless creature maybe without family. [The Russian Revolution has begun.] After the last news that I got from home I realy [sic] fear that my mother will not survive these horrible times. My only fortune is my health and strong will, my brains and strength. They must help me to rebuilt [sic] my life but how long it will take? Is it not strange I never felt before this homelessness. [The next page of the letter is lost.]

N's letters continue sporadically over the next year. He writes to Rose from Tokyo:

I am three days in Tokio, did not see a great deal of it, know just the way from my hotel to different embassies [sic]…Am awfully sorry I cannot wait until the mail arrives, this will be not before the 20th. Nothing to do I have to yield to a "force majeure." Our Ambassador is very nice to me[;] he is an old friend of our family. This Morning he took me in his motorcar for a trip round the city…He told me that it would [be] a shame to leave Tokio without seeing it[;] promised to drive again. I feel I grow old, prefer a[n] early rest to a busy night[.] I even have not any desire to see the well known tea houses and geisha dancers…I carry your picture with me all [the] time[,] just have it now in front of me, write to you looking on it[,] feel as I realy [sic] speak to you. Every time I go back to my hotel from the different offices I visit, I feel so Lonesome and long so ardently you were waiting for me. I close my letter, sweetheart, I feel so sleepy and could not afford another page in English, would surely spoil the letter[,] delaying the posting. Write you soon again. God bless you my darling. Keep off [sic] caring for your loving big N.

The last letter from N. laments the fate of Russia in the Revolution.

I did not have any news from my family since the letter of April the 7. In Petrograd the conditions are so horrible that I have little hope to see my family some days again. Famine, disease, anarchie [sic] are depopulating and ruining completely this ones [sic] blooming happy rich city.

My poor mother[,] how she must suffer, she so patriotic and proud.

Do you remember, Rose, you asked me a year ago why Kastchik [?] was enthusiastic about this damnable revolution and shot. I fore-saw so clearly the coming disaster, but [what] is happening now is twice worse what I expected. We got here precise records that 53,000 officers have been killed by the mob since the revolution started, more than during the war.

Russia has lost now 100,000 of her best class young men (!) and got only dishonor [illegible] and calamities, after having sacrificed for the defeat of Germany more than any other country.

Let us hope that misfortune makes always people stronger and that if not my generation our children will see Russia again great and happy.

Is Dorothy with you[?] I would like to know you with her.

Before I go I write you another letter, my darling, have care of you self, don't forget me.

Your loving friend
N.P.

There is a snapshot of Rose and another woman standing side by side on a street, which was taken, judging by the clothes, in about 1918. Rose is wearing a smart, black straw sailor hat tilted at an angle; her skirt is a pleated black-and-white plaid that comes to within six inches of the ground (it is not yet the 1920s and "Mrs. Smith's" skirts are still long). Rose wears a sash that proclaims in bold letters "Suffrage." The other woman is identified as Mrs. Edith Griffith. It is interesting, and characteristic of Rose, that she would espouse a cause that was both progressive and fashionable and also one in which, practically speaking, she had no direct interest. Women's suffrage had been an active cause since the days of Elizabeth Cady Stanton and Susan B. Anthony in the 1850s. The movement gained force with the new liberation of women during World War I when they served as nurses in France and did other war work that took them out of the parlor. In 1920, the Nineteenth Amendment to the Constitution would finally give women the vote. Rose was liberated and, along with her sisters, would build a groundbreaking independent career. At the same time, her companion in the suffrage demonstration was almost certainly a fashionable society woman whom Rose wanted to know. And, in 1918, Rose was not yet an American citizen, so her marching for the Vote for Women, while stylish and generous, was a gesture made as much for appearances and contacts as from conviction.

The world that would open up in the 1920s was as different from the polite provincial world in which Rose had grown up as jazz was from a teatime cotillion on shipboard. With the old world in a shambles behind her, Rose, wearing her suffragette's sash, marched firmly forward into the twentieth century.

Rose Cumming invented today's clichés. In 1931 I went through a
series of rooms she'd done at the American Art Gallery.
The walls were covered with silver leaf, glazed in brilliant blues,
grape purples, with Directoire furniture covered in gold leaf and
emerald satin. It was rich beyond belief. An ordinary woman
would have disappeared in such a room — but not she.

Edward Wormley,
interior designer writing an obituary of Rose Cumming
in *Home Furnishings Daily*, 1968

OPPOSITE Rose wearing one of the grand picture hats
designed for her by Adrian, Hollywood hatmaker to the stars.
Photograph by Wilbur Pippin, collection of Albert Hadley.

CHAPTER FOUR

Opening the Door

Frank Crowninshield knew what he was doing when he recommended that Rose become a decorator. The cover of *House & Garden* for April, 1917—the month of his and Rose's lunch—shows a fanciful painting of an English cottage with a luxuriant garden in front. Across the bottom of the cover there is a banner announcing "Interior Decoration Number." A few years before there would have been no such issue.

The introductory editorial of the issue tackles the question of the moment head-on. It is titled "What Is Modern Decoration?" The author, B. Russell Herts, is a decorator himself. Herts's first sentence introduces what everyone who remembers her found to be a salient characteristic in Rose's personality: "Modern decoration represents the return of a sense of humor into art." Herts goes on to acknowledge that the profession is in its early stages: "We are in the period of the early seekers; we are the Giottos, the Cimabues, of this century, or rather the unknown strugglers of the pre-natal period; those who render the Giottos and Cimabues possible."

Herts compares the paradoxes evident in contemporary literature and the theater with what is possible in decorating. "It is the age of the immoral moralists, of amusing thinkers, of gay churchmen, and of artists who dare to be inartistic—according to their elders." He continues to deplore the bleaching out of taste and color that early reactions to Victorian clutter produced:

OPPOSITE The cover of the "Interior Decoration Number," April, 1917, *House & Garden*. This was the very month that Rose had her career-making lunch with Frank Crowninshield, when he suggested she become a decorator. *Courtesy of Woodruff/House & Garden; © Condé Nast.*

House & Garden

INTERIOR DECORATION NUMBER

APRIL 1917   CONDÉ NAST & COMPANY inc. Publishers   25 CENTS

We are tired of the eternal preachment of neutral backgrounds, of taupe walls, taupe rugs, cream ceilings, enamel in the bedroom and walnut in the sitting-room and oak in the dining room… We welcome the bizarre, the ridiculous, the vivid exhibitions that would have been reveled in by the very masters of the 15th century, whom we are told to copy, if these men were living today. For the greatest ages of decoration have invariably been vivid, in the colors of art and of life.

Herts goes on to discuss the work of a few decorators and repeats his injunction not just to copy the antique. And then, in his last three paragraphs, he states again that the nascent discipline is in a budding stage and concludes with a ringing manifesto:

Thus far our accomplishments in decoration have been in part imitative, and in part crude, tentative and experimental. We have had insufficient opportunity for original expression; there has been but little encouragement, except in the last couple of years, and then more particularly in the designing of interiors for the stage.

Artists, perceiving in decoration the most untouched and hopeful of the arts, have gone to it from painting and sculpture, and architects, whose interest lay primarily in color and design, rather than in construction, have seen new possibilities in the specialization in interior work.

It is unbelievable, inconceivable, that these influences, this quickened energy, this new stimulus, should lead to nothing but a knowledge of the historic periods, and the willingness to draw from them an endless series of satisfactory and mildly pleasing schemes of line and color. Something new will come, must come, if art is to live; and this will be Modern Decoration.

Both here and earlier in the editorial, much of what Herts says can be applied specifically to Rose's work, particularly in her mature period. The humor, the sense of color, the love of paradox—all of these would come into full flower in Rose's house on West Fifty-third Street.

In these heady, early days of interior design, "Crownie" first sent Rose to work for Mrs. Buel, whom she describes in her essay "A Door Always Open," in the seminal 1964 book *The Finest Rooms by America's Great Decorators*, as "a famous New York decorator at that time." Rose would have learned the nuts and bolts of design with Mrs. Buel. She says in this essay, "I've been decorating…since the day I took my first job and started sorting samples." She would have learned how to make window treatments (or order them)—which one day she would fashion according to her own experimental eye out of such avant-garde materials as cellophane—she would have learned about color (although with Rose's eye, there was little to teach her) and how to deal with clients (high-handedly in Rose's case).

After a year or two, Rose went to Au Quatrième, where she absorbed like a sponge Nancy McClelland's esoteric and particular knowledge about antiques and wallpapers. Decades later, designers such as Albert Hadley and Mario Buatta, who would become icons in their field, remembered walking into Rose's shop when they were young men and having her carefully explain the provenance and significance of rare Boule tables and Chippendale chairs there.

Sometime between 1918 and 1921, Rose got her parents to come from Australia to join her, Dorothy, and Eileen in New York. They lived, according to an envelope forwarded to Rose from Claridge's Hotel in London on August 3, 1921, at 480 Park Avenue.

When the present Grand Central Terminal was built between 1903 and 1913, the New York Central railroad tracks, which had previously run in an open trench down the middle of what is now Park Avenue, were electrified and buried underground. This created some of the most desirable real estate in the world, and, between 1913 and 1930, many of the palatial apartment houses that line Park Avenue were erected. At the corner of East Fifty-eighth Street and Park Avenue, 480 Park Avenue, one of the few remaining residential buildings south of Fifty-ninth Street, was not built until 1929, however. Before that the Hotel Clarendon and some old apartment buildings occupied the site. The Cummings seem to have liked living in hotels (for instance, there are social notes in the *New York Times* through the 1920s that say such things as "Mrs. Victor Cumming and her daughter, Miss

Rose Cumming, are spending the winter at the Plaza Hotel"), so it is likely that their residence at 480 Park Avenue was the Hotel Clarendon.

In 1921, Rose opened her shop. It was on the second floor of a building on Madison Avenue between Forty-sixth and Forty-seventh streets. As she says in "A Door Always Open," the rent money for the first months had been given to her by her sister Dorothy, and "Schmidt Brothers" (as Rose spelled it) had allowed her to take furniture on consignment from their shop. In T*he New York Blue Book—Business Directory* for 1930, under the category "Antiques," there is a listing for "Schmitt Brothers Antiques" at 523 Madison Avenue. These were likely Rose's sponsors.

As we have told earlier, Rose goes on to say in her essay that she had a terrible robbery four months after she opened and lost everything. She was rescued—she says "that very day," although she also says her savior learned of her catastrophe from the newspapers so it seems likely there was at least a day's lag—by an unknown person who sent her a check for $5,000, which was the value of her inventory. How unknown to Rose this benefactor really was is up for question—and we may have some candidates as the story progresses—but, in any case, she was back in business.

As early as August 1918, Rose had gone to England to buy antiques, according to a letter from an Englishwoman saying that Rose's note "with Frank Crowninshield's letter of introduction" had been forwarded to her and she would be back in town the next week and looked forward to seeing Rose. Rose would go to Europe every year for a decade and a half after that, shopping, taking in the atmosphere, and flirting, perhaps, with Arthur Brooke in his flat overlooking Piccadilly and the Green Park.

England in the early 1920s was recovering from the eviscerating loss of the best of a generation of young men in the Great War of 1914–1918. The reaction seems to have been a wish to deny the tragedies that so many families experienced with an immersion among upper-class young people in frolicking, giving parties, and the creation of the myth of "the roaring twenties." The country itself had been scarcely damaged, unlike the pummeling it would receive in World War II, so life in London for a well-funded visitor such as Rose, who was staying at Claridge's, would have been sunny (mostly) and fun during those summers. Rose talks in "A Door Always Open" about being invited to a ball at "the house of the Duchess of Rutland." Her sister Eileen says that in London Rose "would engage a car early in the morning and start out with a chauffeur. They drove all over England's little villages. She'd stop anyplace she wanted. Her friends would tell her what was going to be sold in the great homes."

She traveled and shopped on the Continent as well as in England, and there are glamorous letters of introduction and correspondence with people there as well. There is a letter from this period to H.S.H. (His Serene Highness) Prince Victor v. Thurn and Taxis in Vienna. The prince's was one of the oldest names in the Austro-Hungarian Empire. His correspondent, who writes from 14 East Sixtieth Street, appears to be a relative since the letter is signed "Leila Taxis." She says:

Dear Victor

Miss Rose Cumming is going on some business alone to Vienna & possibly Budapest & I hope you will give her some of your time to accompany her possibly about Vienna or at least to give her the benefit of your knowledge of Vienna.

Another letter is typed in French on paper with the letterhead "Bagues Freres, 107, Rue La Boetie, Bronze, Ferronnerie." The firm apparently sold antique bronzes and ironwork, and the letter thanks Rose for her check for 250 francs and says they hope they can serve her any time she needs them. That Rose was already buying fabric is attested to in a P.S. that says that they are confirming their telegram of yesterday in which they told her that "la maison Matthieu" was able to furnish the fabric ("le tissu") she wanted at 17.50 francs per meter.

The letter is dated September 19, 1922, not long after Rose arrived home on the *Majestic*, according to her entry records at Ellis Island, and it has a postscript written by hand in English. The business-like body of the letter combined with the

73

A bedroom on East Fifty-fifth Street
decorated by Rose. The painted walls and
satin pillows were favorite devices of hers.
Collection of the New-York Historical Society,
Matte E. Hewitt and Richard A. Smith Collection.

An Old Brownstone Building Transformed

A House in which the Decorator Had the Unusual Opportunity of Designing and Furnishing a Home for Herself, Indulging for Once All Her Own Tastes and Fancies.

Third in a Series by Women Decorators

By ROSE CUMMING

Rose Cumming, Decorator   *Photographs by G. W. Harting*

THE decorations and furnishings of a house must necessarily depend so much upon the house itself, that I was discouraged when I found that the only vacant houses in the neighborhood of my shop were old-fashioned and unsuitable in many respects.

The narrow old brownstone building which I eventually acquired on account of its accessible position was in a state of fearful dilapidation, and it was not easy to visualize it as a restored and pleasant habitation. Its condition, however, gave me the excuse I wanted to alter and reconstruct some of the rooms without the necessity of destroying anything beautiful in the process.

My idea in decorating the house was to make it redolent of the eighteenth century as it expresses itself in England, to some extent; but also the eighteenth century of other countries as well. I did not wish to be tied down too strictly to any particular style or period. Why not have my house embody all that I had most admired in my travels about the world?

So I drew up my plans without too much

formality, and in less than three months had moved in my choicest treasures and had prosecuted my search for suitable materials and furnishings to such good purpose that there were very few gaps to fill. Of course I have since made alterations—taken away here and added there—but the whole remains essentially the same, and I like to think that I have been successful in creating here in the heart of New York something a little like one of the old houses one meets in London.

Furnishing, however, was not easy, as in many cases the proportions were difficult and far from good. Take for instance the hall. I feel that upon entering a house one should at once be made conscious of the dominant note pervading its scheme of decoration. This was difficult as the hall was narrow and irregular. Eventually the chief problem was met by placing a large coromandel screen near the foot of the staircase, and by hanging on the opposite wall an old painting of a family group which is so completely domestic in every detail, from the Nubian slave down to the pet squirrel in the corner, that it has always

Right—A very fine Queen Anne secretary in red lacquer brings a warm color note into the library the same lively tones appearing in a large Persian rug

Below—Antique chintz curtains and draw curtains of peach taffeta are used effectively with apple green walls and bois de rose carpet in this colorful boudoir

Above—Silver leaf and mirror bandings give added fascination to the unusual design of this bed by Rose Cumming. The old embroidered satin spread repeats the soft Chinese colorings used throughout furnishing and mural decoration

ABOVE In an *Arts & Decoration* magazine article from 1928, Rose wrote about her first transformation of the house on West Fifty-third Street, which would be the showcase for her talent and where she would live for the next 35 years. *Arts & Decoration*, May 1928. *Art & Architecture Collection, Miriam and Ira D. Wallach Division of Art, Prints and Photographs, the New York Public Library, Astor, Lenox and Tilden Foundations.*

The dining room opens directly on a garden, the freshness of which enters into the gray-green, apricot and silver interior. A scenic paper is used and the furniture is Chippendale

struck me as being particularly quaint and amusing. The warm colors of this picture serve to relieve the sombreness of the walls which are of wrapping paper, brown, and I have also tried to get a lively feeling by painting the woodwork and the staircase lacquer red.

An old refectory table, standing beneath the picture, bought from the Dowager Duchess of Sutherland, is one of my most treasured possessions; a sacred Chinese apple tree of the Ming period, nearby, tempts all comers with its harvest of luscious golden fruit, like the tree in the garden of the Hesperides that Hercules plundered. But my apples are better guarded for there are two raging dragons instead of one to threaten the unwary offender—albeit they are but of Chinese porcelain.

At the far end of the hall is my library. This room was used as a dining room by the previous owners, but I have transferred the dining room to the basement by taking out all the old fittings of the kitchen and converting that into a very comfortable room. The library is oblong with eight walls—an unusual shape that lent itself to a very attractive scheme of decoration. On the two narrow walls either side of the folding doors I covered built-in bookshelves. At the other end I was faced with the ill balanced problem of two windows and a door leading into the one-time butler's pantry which is now a little dressing room. These I treated, all alike, as windows in order to preserve the general balance, and curtained them with long

(Continued on page 102)

English XVIIIth Century furniture in the library includes Chippendale and Queen Anne with some Louis XIIIth chairs giving variety in form and color

Library walls are jade green and the rug a rare old Khorassan with animal design, the motif repeated in several very fine porcelain figures

This room is identified in Rose's article, "An Old Brownstone Building Transformed" of May, 1928, as a "Venetian guest room ... decorated in green, yellow and peach and the shell-like bed is said to have belonged to Napoleon's sister." *Dessin Fournir Collections.*

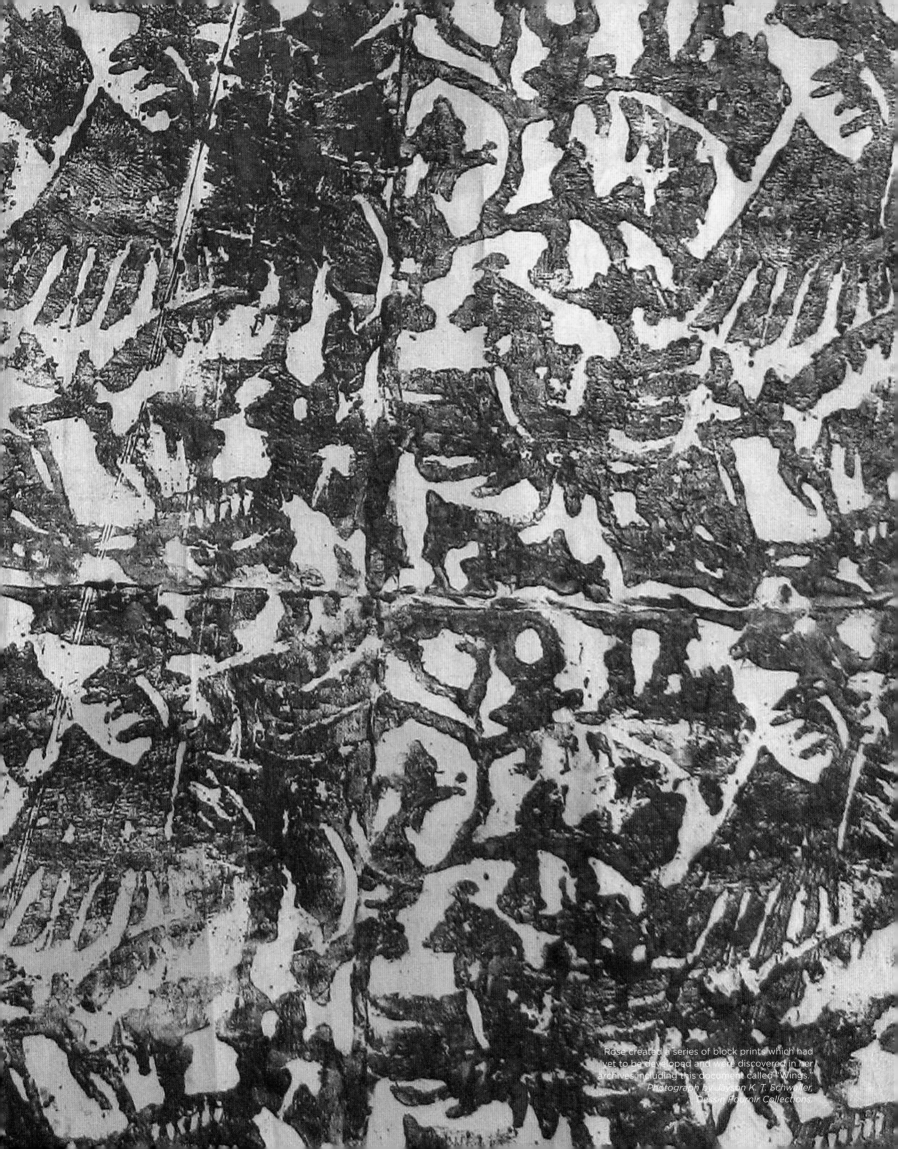

Rose created a series of block prints which had yet to be developed and were discovered in her archives including this document called "Wings." Photograph by Jayson K. T. Schweller, Dessin Fournir Collections

An Old Brownstone Building Transformed

(Continued from page 61)

hangings of an antique red satin. I have used a real jade green for the walls of the library, and since the ceiling is exceptionally high I decided to treat it with the same color. This exact shade can only be produced by the use of a certain very vivid green washed over with Prussian blue.

Queen Anne secretary; but here and there I have introduced a chair of the Louis XIII period which is so closely akin to the Jacobean.

The ornaments are rather masculine in type: a pair of old Persian tiles, alabaster horses from Burma, lanterns from China, antique Persian

The Venetian guest room is decorated in green, yellow and peach and the shell-like bed is said to have belonged to Napoleon's sister

Since the walls and the curtains are plain, I have introduced a good deal of design into the rugs and accessories and some of the upholstery. The large rug in the centre, a rare old Khorassan which was given by the late Sultan of Turkey to a one-time military attaché, has an unusual animal design

lacquer boxes, bits of old Staffordshire pottery and painted lamp shades; while the pictures include two large portraits by Sir William Beechey R. A., one of William IV when he was Duke of Clarence, and the other of Admiral Maitland upon whose ship Napoleon was conveyed a prisoner to

The bathroom is lapis blue and the large mirror is decorated behind the glass in blue and green design, a revival of an old art

in which deer, rabbits and tigers chase each other over a red and jade-green ground, and this motif is repeated in the chimerean porcelain figures placed about the room.

The furniture is mostly of the English eighteenth century, including some Chippendale and a very fine

Elba. The two mirrors in gilt frames, hanging on either side of the chimney-piece, were presented by George II to the Earl of Stafford.

The dining room, which was the original basement kitchen, has a door leading into the garden, and is reached

(Continued on page 104)

An Old Brownstone Building Transformed

(Continued from page 102)

from the first floor by way of the old back staircase which I endeavored to make attractive by hanging a set of vivid old hunting prints upon the fresh-green walls.

The ceiling in the dining room is so low that it was not practical to use pictures, and in order to impart some interest and beauty to the room I papered the walls with one of the famous Zuber hand-blocked papers entitled "Scenic America". There is just one picture, however, a portrait of a lady which seemed to harmonize so well with the spirit of the room that I could not deny her a place above the mantlepiece.

The dining room furniture is Chippendale; its low build making it particularly suitable to the proportions of the room. There are dark apricot-colored satin curtains, a gray-green carpet and a silver screen, and, as in every other room in the house, there is something that I rejoice in more than in anything else—an open hearth.

In my experience of decorating I have found that people often hesitate before they will introduce blue into the color scheme of a room, especially that shade—the bright, rich blue that is used so much in pictures of the Madonna—which has always been my favorite color. So I determined to have a room in my own house which would demonstrate my theory that this color really can be used with good effect. The little blue French drawing-room, on the entrance side of the hall, was designed to house the thousand and one useless and charming odds and ends that are so beloved in Europe though so little used here.

Of the many curios which have found a home in this room, my favorite is a small Louis XVI table which had evidently been sent to Venice to be inlaid, for there is a border of ivory of such surprisingly intricate design that it has the appearance of old lace. There are several pieces from the collection of the Dowager Duchess of Sutherland, and I am also very much attached to an old china dog that sits by the fire in his flowered coat, and to a little silver mandarin designed to hold toothpicks between the spokes of his parasol.

When thinking out my bedroom I decided to fashion a little dream world, a kingdom of unreality, so that every night when I crossed the magic threshold I should feel myself in another and rarified existence.

Without the help of Mr. Arnnof, the Russian artist, my plan would never have reached perfection; he grasped my idea at once, and when I explained to him that a Chinese mandarin figure, which I had loved and carried about with me since I was a child must be the inspiration of the whole design, he executed a mural decoration which expressed the mandarin's dream.

In furnishing this room I tried to achieve something which had the charm of the antique, yet in simplicity and clearness of colors would savor of the feeling of modernism without being actually modernistic. The bed, made from my own design, is finished with silver leaf, with mirror bandings on the outsides of the rails, footboard and top, and with an old Chinese spread of silver colored satin embroidered with flowers. Soft Chinese colorings are used through-

out: On either side of the bed is a tall stand of Chinese Chippendale of robin's egg blue, and these in their turn are flanked by a pair of modern consoles, to which I am devoted.

Leading out of my bedroom there is a little dressing room of irregular design. The signs of the Zodiac are used as the motif for the decoration here, and there are black walls spangled with golden stars, a gold painted ceiling and a black floor covered with a rug of emu feathers.

My bathroom is certainly changed from the white tiled room I found when I took over the house. It is now entirely lapis blue; the tiles, the marbleized walls, and the bath itself are all carried out in this lovely color, and on the wall above the bath is a large mirror with a blue and green design painted behind the glass.

My sitting room is on this floor and here I intended above all to convey a sense of comfort and to bring together the colors I like best, so I introduced some easy chairs and a comfortable couch upholstered in violet satin. Several family portraits hang on these walls as well as a fine example of Allan Ramsay's work and a painting by Thomas Bardwell of his daughter, in which the dress is just the right shade of blue to harmonize with the blue-green taffeta curtains. I should also like to draw attention to the four wood carvings on the wall which came from the Earl of Stafford's family and are among the finest examples I have ever seen of such work, of the Louis XVI period.

On the next floor are my mother's rooms which are much more conventional in type. In the bedroom the walls and dressing-table are of a very soft blue-green, and I was lucky enough to find an old directoire bed in France two years ago which exactly suited these surroundings, and which I have draped in silk of that beautiful shade known as cosmos pink. The carpet is soft lilac, and on the antique directoire chairs are coverings of chintz with a design of lilac sprays.

Naturally a house of this type is very far removed from the needs of most people. I have been able to indulge many little eccentricities that I have to suppress in business but I think it has a certain interest in that to give it a different aspect.

You have asked me how long it took me to complete my house. I will answer that with a question. "Is a house ever quite finished?" Hardly a day passes that some detail is not changed. I find a picture fits a certain place better than the present one, or I acquire a perfectly delightful new chair and room has to be found for it. No, I don't think my house will ever really be completed. The skeleton, however, I accomplished very quickly. I think it was remodeled, painted, papered, curtained with all the furniture moved in in ten weeks, even though it was early fall and a busy season for us all. The matter of speed is chiefly a matter of correct visualization. If you have a complete vision of the finished room before you begin, it is fairly easy to get all the different wheels moving without loss of time. It is usually in the seemingly unimportant details that we agonize and fail and succeed, perhaps to fail again, but it's a fascinating business— the business of creating beauty with real rewards when things go right.

An opulent bathroom in lapis lazuli and etched glass.
Dessin Fournir Collections.

postscript shows how Rose combined her flirtations, her social climbing, and her business on her travels. The postscript says: "Still contemplate being over in November. I know Mr. Duke of St. Alban is simply crazy to see you. Between you and me I am afraid he is in love with you." It is possible, of course, that Mr. Duke of St. Alban was a dog, but the letter is still a charming combination of business and flirtatiousness. Just how far Rose's flirtatiousness went is up for questioning, but there is a letter sent by "Guillermo" from Paris one September in the 1920s that would seem to spell things out.

My dear Rose

Today is just a week you left, and I am missing you very much. When I go through the Place Vendôme, I look with some melancholy the Hotel du Rhin, and think at the very short but nice moments we spent there … I just have the idea of the dream that it was—

Rose, I kant [sic] kiss you and love, just nothing—Better not to say anything—What for?

Good bye Rose. Recive [sic] all my love and don't forget your for darling

Guillermo

Examples of the important antiques that Rose bought during the 1920s from a fairly wide range of periods can be inferred from the catalogue and articles about an auction of her inventory, which took place in 1932.

According to *ARTnews* magazine, the most important piece in the collection was an interior in carved pine wainscoting by William Kent that was brought from Calcote [sic] Park, Reading, England: *This ensemble, consisting of a drawing room with four doors and three windows, ranks as one of the most important paneled rooms in this country. Details in which this architect's genius are particularly apparent are the superb carving and design of the door pediment and the acanthus-flanked mantel, with amorini mask in the center.*

There are several interesting points about this attribution. The room certainly is a carved and paneled eighteenth-century interior. And it may well have come from Calcot Park

(not "Calcote"), near Reading in England, all the more because, in 1929, when Rose was making annual trips to Europe and was in high-acquisition mode, Calcot Park was bought from the family who had owned it since the mid-eighteenth century by a group of Reading businessmen. They created a golf course on the grounds and used the house as a club house. They had to raise £19,500 to buy the estate and another £5,000 to lay out the golf course, so what more likely than to sell the period interior decoration.

The problem with attributing the room to William Kent, however, who was an illustrious eighteenth-century English painter, architect, designer of interiors, designer of furniture, and landscape architect, is that Kent died in 1748. The Calcot Park House, which still exists and from which Rose's paneled room would have come, replaced an earlier house on the site and was not built until 1759.

It would be typical of Rose, in her intrepid pursuit of antiques that she often could not afford but loved, to dress up the provenance a little bit, just as she in later life dressed up her already wonderful and appealing antique self with fringe on the Adrian hats and more and more scarves and jewelry. Among other items in the auction inventory of 1932 is a Florentine fireplace surround of white Carrara marble with caryatids supporting the mantel; a set of Sheraton dining chairs; a Louis XV walnut sofa upholstered in the original needlework is attributed to Cressant; and a gilded Hispano-Moresque wrought-iron gate, which may well have come from Bagues Freres, who specialized in bronze and "ferronnerie."

Most interestingly, perhaps, in light of Rose's enduring reputation, *ARTnews* notes in this inventory of European purchases that "The high decorative quality of antique, painted wallpapers, both European and Oriental, has made them greatly in demand by collectors. Miss Cumming offers on this occasion a fine series of such papers, including some historical Chinese specimens." The lessons from Nancy McClelland at Au Quatrième were not lost.

Finally, again as a forecast of the coming decades, the "textiles include a wide range of hangings, cushions and table covers in antique Spanish, French and Italian brocades, velvets and damasks."

The late Mark Hampton, in his book *Legendary Decorators of the Twentieth Century* (1992), makes a fascinating point about Rose's work with textiles. After talking about her unique eye as a colorist that he says, "enabled her to produce the beautiful chintzes that carry her name to this day," he continues:

She was also a great lover of old materials, an element of decorating now difficult to pursue because of their scarcity. But sixty years ago [he is writing in 1992] it was possible to lay your hands on any number of old brocades, velvets, and painted silks, all of which Rose used with great enthusiasm. We must not forget that McKim, Mead & White were able…to go to Italy and find sufficient yardage of antique Genoese velvet to upholster entire rooms — walls, furniture, and curtains — enabling them to give a room an instant atmosphere of the past. Rose liked this atmosphere of age and decay, though she would juxtapose elements of faded deterioration with shiny wall surfaces and mirrors so that the ancient quality of the materials never gave that dusty feeling of a room preserved from the past. Her rooms were definitely of the present.

Some light is shone on Rose's shopping methods in Europe by a series of letters from a French beau named Jacques. Jacques seems to have been a version of the Russian beau of a few years before — sweetly sincere, a mix of sophistication and naïveté, and communicating in fractured English, for which he apologizes.

On "Samedi 4 Septembre 1926" he writes:

Rose,

When your boat begin to move away, I had a physical pain like I never could imagine — it was like if my hart [sic] was in your hands and only a small vein between and when the boat disappeared I cannot tell you what I feel. All that must seem strange to you, it is for me too, but I understand because here we feel more stronger [sic] I think. Best beloved, I had yesterday written a long letter, but I think it is better to destroy it: my love for you was to [sic] big in it. I had too day [sic] your darling letter of Portsmouth. It gave such a joy that it is the first day I am able to run my ordinary life. You tell me that I must know what you have in your heart because it is quite impossible for you to write it. Dearest, it is so sweet for me to read it!! And you see I don't agree with you — what will happen if two people loving each other would think impossible to tell their love?

Really, Rose, it is a great punishment for me that I am not able to explain me better in English. I would like to tell you my loneliness and wanting for you: they are quite unbearable.

I have got your frame after a big discussion for 6000 francs. I have found a very small elephant make by a great sculpteur [sic]. I hope it please you. I had difficulties to send it because of the gold.

Write me, Rose beloved, not two pages with only few words, but a letter telling me many things of you: it mean so much for me!

I am your [sic] entirely
Jacques

Two days later, on "6 Septembre," Jacques writes again:

Rose,

I have for you adoration like for god and love like for a woman.

Since you left I could not recover from this sad feeling of extreme loneliness. I feel I can do anything easily when you are near me, but without you…I hope it will pass away. Saturday and yesterday I have done again but alone the same thing that we have done last week. I was at [illegible] and have seen again the dear places.

Don't tell me I am crazy or made [sic]. I am strong but love you with all my being and I am French.

The seller of the frame call on me today to tell me that Mr. de la Raucher…[name lost] answered him that he had no money to pay for you: I done the necessary and send the bill in order in the case of need for you.

Doing something for you, my only one, give me a little sweetness. I am longing for your letters: not letter official and polite, but letters of your heart if I like and hope has still something for me — Rose best beloved I cant [sic] tell you more than those four words with their full signification, I belong to you Jacques. If I read again this letter I will never send her: I feel is a child's letter, but I kan't [sic] write in English — forgive me —

There are three more letters from Jacques — one from "21 Décembre 1926," one from "29 Mars 1927," and one from "27

Août 1928." In the December 1926 letter, Jacques bemoans that he cannot be with Rose for Christmas. "How I would like to be near you for Christmas, to tell you sweet thinks [sic], to love you … I need so much to see you." He has sent her a gold box for a Christmas present, which, because of export limitations on gold, he has declared at a low value, but—ever the practical French businessman—"I have got an insurance for the full value."

Rose's father, Victor Cumming, had died in 1926, at the age of 65, while staying with Dorothy in California. Jacques says in his letter of March 29, 1927, "I was very sick in England when I heard that your dear Father died: I was very sad for you and I remembered the care you take for his billets etc [his letters?] and it seemed to me that I had know [sic] him…"

In the next paragraph, Jacques touches on an important aspect of Rose's personality according to many people who knew her—her generosity. "Remember the night when you found the poor man in the Champs-Élysées and all you have done for him and he was unknow [sic] to you and your good heart pushed you…" Jacques goes on to complain that she is less generous to him—"you could have made me happy with one word every month"—and then he debates about going to New York—"I maybe oblige to go to New York for a zociety [sic] of whom I am Prasident [sic]."

Jacques did not go to New York, although in August of 1928 he apparently met Rose and her mother in Paris. This, the last letter from him that we have, ends on the slightly distanced note that we have come to recognize as typical of the correspondence from Rose's suitors when they have been kept dangling too long.

Dearest Rose,

What a sad summer for me—everything seemed to keep me away from you—the business and my bad moud [sic] and your difficulty to be alone—And I wanted so much to be with you, perhaps much more than ever. You are the only one women that I feel zo comprehensive, zo true, and zo good. I admire you deeply, Rose.

RIGHT In a day when there was no negative feeling about using animal skins for decoration, Rose, bringing in a breath of the wild, combined a tiger skin rug and a bear skin rug with her signature sinuous satin draperies and upholstery. *Photograph by G. W. Harting, Dessin Fournir Collections.*

By the way I don't admire your perpetual rushing!!!

I was very happy to know your Mother — she charming and certainly a lady. Now I know better your family and I am more able to zee you in your ordinary life.

What will be the future? I really don't know! I will keep you posted with the principal news.

Godbye [sic], zweet dear Rose, all my tenderness for you.
Jacques

Leaving her suitors, other letters from 1928 suggest this is a good year to look at how Rose has now shaped her life personally and professionally. As we have said, her generosity (to everyone except suitors perhaps) was a hallmark of Rose's life. Relatives — from an aunt in Australia to Dorothy's son, Anthony Cumming, living today in Albuquerque, New Mexico friends, and virtual strangers underscore the point. Aunt Anne writes from Australia in the 1920s, mentioning "Dorrie's and Eily's babies" — Dorothy's two sons and Eileen's one son were all born in the 1920s — then she says: "Thanks dear for the parcel & cheque — you know you are a darling girl to remember me all these miles away." In the next letter, Aunt Anne takes a sterner and more concerned tone:

We have always appreciated all you have done for us. It has been such a tremendous lot — more perhaps than you realize — but I have always felt that the special Xmas present was perhaps a drain — I never liked to say anything — you understand, don't you darling but I just hoped that you would not embarrass yourself to send [it] — I know what I am myself and so I understand you — always trying to do too much and worrying accordingly — you are burdened with excessive good nature and unfortunately it is not always returned — I have wanted for ages past to say a lot in my letters but have refrained because you are so much cleverer than I; but I have many more years of life experience so can see what you can't that there comes a time when it is folly not to put oneself first — you aren't getting any younger and you should shut your purse and beyond your dear Mother there should be no money spent nor given away — now darling forgive me for this lecture if it makes you pause and think I won't mind if it also vexes you but you don't know how I worry over you.

But it is not only to relatives that Rose's generosity extends. On April 16, 1928, a young man named George Buchwald

wrote to her from the Hotel Manger in New York.

Dear Miss Cumming,

I hardly know just how to express my profound gratitude to you for your wonderfully sportsman-like action this afternoon. When I left your place I thanked you in a sort of perfunctory manner because there were others about and I can't help feeling that it sounded a bit smug — I mean that it seemed as though I considered the whole transaction a sort of normal business deal — you advanced me some money against security. Now, I want to earnestly emphasize my real feelings, because I know perfectly well that that beastly lace is of no earthly use to you whereas cash is cash and I appreciate the pure sportsmanship of your act very deeply, more in fact, than I can express. It wasn't merely helping a lame dog over a stile, you got me out of the very devil of a hole and I now have breathing space to attend to my business of landing a job.

And on August 30, 1928, a woman named Katherine Lethbridge wrote to Rose from London saying that she had just seen Dorothy and Rose's mother and was sorry to miss seeing Rose by one day. Katherine Lethbridge says, "My dear I've had some very bad news since last I saw you & the picture looks [illegible] black unless I could get some real work .... Now my request is this do you think you could find me a niche [?] in your big business…I believe I do get on with people especially Americans…" There's no knowing whether Rose found a place for Katherine Lethbridge, but clearly Rose was a refuge in time of trouble, often anticipating the needs of the objects of her charity before they stated them.

These examples of Rose's personal generosity indicate she had achieved a level of financial independence, making 1928 also a good year to pause for a look at her creative and professional development. *Arts & Decoration*, the magazine that sponsored Nancy McClelland's home study course on interior decoration, which Rose would have known about and may have participated in ten years earlier, has an article by Rose in the May 1928 issue, "An Old Brownstone Building Transformed." The subhead of the article is "A House in which the Decorator Had the Unusual Opportunity of Designing and Furnishing a Home for Herself, Indulging for Once All Her Own Tastes and Fancies." This was Rose's house on West Fifty-third Street, where she would live for 35 years and which would become her manifesto of design and a wonder to all who saw it.

In 1928, she had not yet gotten to the point of making it Shangri-la. There were still elements of the conservative traditional English style of her first work, but the basics and some distinguishing touches were there.

Rose begins by saying:

The narrow old brownstone building which I eventually acquired on account of its accessible position was in a state of fearful dilapidation, and it was not easy to visualize it as a restored and pleasant habitation. Its condition, however, gave me the excuse I wanted to alter and reconstruct some of the rooms without the necessity of destroying anything beautiful in the process. My idea in decorating the house was to make it redolent of the eighteenth century as it expresses itself in England, to some extent; but also the eighteenth century of other countries as well. I did not wish to be tied down too strictly to any particular style or period. Why not have my house embody all that I had most admired in my travels about the world?

Rose goes on to talk about the difficult proportions in the house and says,

Take, for instance, the hall. I feel that upon entering a house one should at once be made conscious of the dominant note pervading its scheme of decoration. This was difficult as the hall was narrow and irregular. Eventually the chief problem was met by placing a large coromandel screen near the foot of the staircase, and by hanging on the opposite wall an old painting of a family group which is so completely domestic in every detail, from the Nubian slave down to the tiny pet squirrel in the corner, that it has always struck me as being particularly quaint and amusing. The warm colors of this picture serve to relieve the sombreness of the walls which are of wrapping paper, brown, and I have also tried to get a lively feeling by painting the woodwork and the staircase lacquer red.

Rose's cavalier attitude about combining things she liked, regardless of seeming suitability, is evident in the walls of brown wrapping paper, the screen, the family portrait and the red lacquer woodwork.

She also mentions a refectory table that she had bought from Millicent, the Dowager Duchess of Sutherland, a favorite figure in Rose's pantheon. Acknowledging this favoritism, Mark Hampton notes in *Legendary Decorators of the Twentieth Century*:

Rose had spent a great deal of time in England and spoke always of the great Edwardian hostesses as though they would come through the door at any minute. One of her idols was the famous Millicent Sutherland, the subject of the great Sargent portrait that hung for years in the stairway of Ben Sonnenberg's house. To see that Sargent portrait and realize she was one of Rose's ideals is to grasp immediately the ethos of Rose's glamorous, dashing style. Her preference in furniture and accessories was always for things of great beauty, but with a slightly mannered twist, which she intensified by the way in which she combined them.

In addition to the table, Rose owned a number of pieces of furniture, the provenance of which she attributed to the duchess, the implication being that Rose knew her more or less well and hence had entrée into such fashionable social enclaves.

Rose also talks about her library in this piece in a way that suggests by 1928 she had attained the colorful high style that visitors remember from many years later. She says, "I have used a real jade green for the walls of the library…This exact shade can only be produced by the use of a certain very vivid green washed over with Prussian blue. Since the walls…are plain, I have introduced a good deal of design into the rugs." She also mentions a Queen Anne secretary, which was red japanned lacquer.

Mark Hampton on the library:

The back room, which was the library, was painted a rich, dark green, a color halfway between that of an emerald and lush summer grass. The sofa was covered in purple satin, a typical Rose touch. She loved satin and purple. A set of red lacquer chairs clashed admirably with the purple sofa. On the floor were two or three Chinese carpets in blue and yellow. You can imagine the shock of these colors—brilliant green, brilliant purple, brilliant red, and blue and yellow carpets. The ancientness of all the surfaces—the wood, the paint and the carpets—gave the room a mellow softness that was completely satisfying without being in the least jarring.

Rose, with her fondness for a provenance that is sometimes too fabulous to believe, identifies one of the rugs, "a rare old Khorassan," as a gift "given by the late Sultan of Turkey to a one-time military attaché." A portrait in the room she says was "by Sir William Beechey…of Admiral Maitland upon whose ship Napoleon was conveyed a prisoner to Elba."

There are several significant omissions in Rose's description of her house in this article, which we can assume simply means that she had not found them yet—or found their place in her aesthetic. One is the magical silver antique Chinese wallpaper in the drawing room; another, which would be a product of her Deco phase in the 1930s, is the silver-blue foil on the walls of her bedroom with the silver lamé draperies in that room; and a third are the tiny squares of mercury glass mirror held together with bronze rosettes and set into Louis XV painted boiserie in the dining room. These, Rose said, had belonged to Daisy Fellowes, a high fashion figure of the first half of the twentieth century, who was an heiress to the Singer sewing machine fortune, a patron of Elsa Schiaparelli, and one-time editor in chief of the French *Harper's Bazaar*.

In 1929, Rose wrote her definition of the career in which she was well ensconced.

Interior decorating is the frivolous sister of the architectural profession. It requires primarily that one be an expert in color, design, period, and the placing of furniture. Most of us have added some knowledge of architecture to our equipment as decorators, so that being conversant with the laws of proportion, line, etcetera, we can intelligently interpret the original design of the architect. A decorator should, in addition, be blessed with a sixth sense—a kind of artistic alchemy which endows the articles of furniture with the elusive quality of liveableness which transforms houses into homes. No amount of training or schooling, I believe, can teach you this. Either you have a flair or you haven't.

RIGHT A portrait of Millicent, Duchess of Sutherland (later Lady Millicent Hawes), painted in 1904 by John Singer Sargent. Rose always implied that she knew the duchess, who was a favorite figure of hers. Mark Hampton wrote: "To see that ... portrait and realize she was one of Rose's ideals is to grasp immediately the ethos of Rose's glamorous, dashing style."
Copyright © Museo Thyssen-Bornemisza. Madrid.

OPPOSITE A print of a portrait of Rose, done in the early 1920s by Otho Cushing (1871–1942), a portrait painter, watercolorist, and caricaturist for *Life* when it was a humor magazine. This portrait was discovered by Robert Mahony of Oakton, Virginia. He was refinishing a chair and found it under the seat cushion.
Courtesy of Robert Mahony.

Miss Rose Cumming

Portrait in Pastel

By

Otho Cushing

*The cottage was eighteenth century, so of course
Rose had to say that it was seventeenth century.*

Russell Cecil,
architect and Rose Cumming's nephew

CHAPTER FIVE

The Social Whirl

There is a letter from this time written to Dorothy in California by a friend of hers named Peggy, who lived at 125 West Eleventh Street, that gives a telling glimpse of Rose in her prime. She wrote, "Rose and Eileen came to a musicale we had on Sunday night, Rose looking too beautiful in a lavender satin gown with a green wreath around her hair. Everybody asked about her and wanted to meet her."

Rose mixed up her social life, her professional life—and her personal life. Most decorators and designers do the same. Social contacts lead to people seeing the decorator's house or houses the decorator has done in the line of business, and professional contacts lead to more commissions—one recommends one's friends—and sometimes to friendships. But Rose did it more than most. She was always, to put it bluntly, on the make, albeit in a delightful way.

A good example of this kind of interconnection is related to two photographs and a short item in the March 1926 *Arts & Decoration*. Although Rose's work appeared frequently in *House & Garden*, *Arts & Decoration* was her reliable showcase from the days when she was first learning her trade. The photographs in the March 1926 issue are part of a collection called "A Group of Distinguished Rooms." One of the captions reads:

Boudoir in the New York apartment of Mrs. Emil J. Stehli in which a rarely beautiful color scheme has been worked out with antique furniture and modern draperies. The window shades are painted linen, the curtains Empire yellow taffeta with fringe in three colors, black, green and yellow, hang under Directoire cornices. Rose Cumming, Decorator

The caption for the second picture says,

In the same boudoir the doors are gold and black in a most effective design. One antique Empire chair is covered in yellow satin and the other is delicate green. The half table between the doors is an interesting Empire design and the paintings, busts, fans, etc. are all in the period. Rose Cumming, Decorator

It is worth noting that Rose's color scheme is lauded. As early as 1926, she was beginning to hit her stride with the lush bold colors that would ultimately become her signature.

Mrs. Emil Stehli, to whom the boudoir with the Empire yellow satin and taffeta and black cornices belonged, was born Marguerite Zweifel in Switzerland, and she was the wife of Emil J. Stehli, also Swiss born. Emil Stehli was a scion of E. Stehli, Sirt & Son, a silk manufacturing firm that originated in Switzerland but operated in the United States. He was the president of the United States Silk Testing Association, as well as president of Stehli & Company, Textile Merchants. Emil Stehli's son, Henry, would succeed his father and broaden the silk testing company's field of operation to include general textile testing. Henry would become chairman of the American Council of Style and Design.

It is easy to see how Rose knew these people professionally as suppliers and associates in business organizations, and how the publicizing of her work would also promote their products. Most likely, after the photographs appeared in *Arts & Decoration*, the next time Rose wanted some silk or taffeta from Stehli & Company, Textile Merchants, for a job, she got a very good mark down indeed.

One source of very lucrative—and in this case glamorous and high profile—contacts for Rose was her youngest sister, Dorothy. Of the three Cumming sisters, as we have said, Rose was the oldest, Eileen was the middle sister, and Dorothy was the youngest. A half-sister, Margery Hughes, a child of Mrs. Cumming's first marriage, crops up in letters from time to time and later would figure in Rose's life in New York. Eileen, by all accounts, although not devoid of glamour and

accomplishment herself—she was the first publicity director for Saks Fifth Avenue when it opened in 1925—was the stable one. Eileen married a rheumatologist, Dr. Russell Cecil, who wrote a textbook, *Cecil's Textbook of Medicine*, which remains a fixture in medical schools. It was Eileen who maintained a home on East Fifty-eighth Street, a refuge for her sisters from time to time, as well as a residence for her husband and son. Dorothy, however, lit the fires under the whole family. It was she who brought Rose and Eileen to New York; it was she who introduced Rose to Frank Crowninshield in 1917; and it was she who, with her very successful career in silent films in the 1920s, introduced Rose to the movie crowd.

Joanne Creveling, a New York publicist with a long career in the design world, says, "I always felt that Dorothy was whispering in Rose's ear."

Dorothy made 39 films between 1915 and 1939, a few in Australia but most of them in the United States. One of the best known was Cecil B. DeMille's *The King of Kings* in 1927, in which she plays Mary, the mother of Jesus. The movie is about the last weeks of Jesus's life before his crucifixion. It boasts many innovative features, including the use of Technicolor in the last sequences, which shows Jesus' Resurrection. DeMille pulled out all of his customary stops for this film and a few more. Mary Magdalene rides out to meet Judas, who is presented as her paramour, in a chariot drawn by zebras, and demons are cast out of Mary Magdalene in a multiple exposure sequence.

Otto Kahn, the world famous financier who played a veiled but crucial part in Rose's story, was involved in the development of the film industry. He was on the board of directors of Paramount, the film company created by Adolph Zukor, who had produced *Snow White*, Dorothy Cumming's first American film in 1916. On September 1, 1926, Kahn left New York with ten guests, including Frank Crowninshield and Condé Nast, traveling in three private railroad cars with three valets, two black chefs, and a courier from the travel agency. There was another private car for the domestic staff and the luggage. The trip, which would take two months and cover 11,708 miles, had Hollywood as a destination point. While there Kahn and his party were taken through the lot of *The King of Kings* by DeMille.

"I had two thousand, five hundred extras in that one scene," de Mille said. "What do you say to that, Mr. Kahn?" "Nothing," said Kahn. "Have you ever seen Velasquez' *Surrender of Breda?* That canvas looks as if it has twenty-five hundred soldiers in it; but when you count the spears, you find there are exactly eighteen of them. And that, Mr. de Mille, is art!"

Mary Jane Matz, in her biography, *The Many Lives of Otto Kahn*, describes Kahn thus:

Clemenceau called Otto Kahn the greatest living American. Thomas Edison thought him one of the most distinguished men in the world. To…Will Rogers he was the "King of New York."

Banker, builder of railroad empires, tireless reader, first-nighter, friend of kings, ministers, presidents, and struggling Greenwich Village artists, captain of the advance legions of liberalism, floater of transatlantic loans, golfer, jester, bon vivant hedonist and lover of beauty in all its forms….[Kahn was the] lifegiver of art in the United States.

As well as a great financier and patron of the arts, Kahn was a great ladies' man. On this trip, he was photographed holding hands with Mary Astor, the two of them sitting in adjacent director's chairs. Kahn liked his love affairs to be in the arts. Despite many years of an amiable marriage and four children, he had a mistress, Marie Jeritza, whose career he furthered as a singer at the Metropolitan Opera.

It can be said with assurance that on the 1926 trip to California Kahn would have met Dorothy Cumming, who was one of the stars of *The King of Kings*: Frank Crowninshield, an old friend of Dorothy's was in the party; and Adolph Zukor, who had produced Dorothy's first American film, and Kahn were colleagues at Paramount. Introductions would have been inevitable, particularly if Dorothy had anything to do with it. Dorothy was as much of a networker as Rose, and, as we know, she frequently passed on useful acquaintances to Rose—for instance, Frank Crowninshield. It is even possible

that Rose was in California during Otto Kahn's visit. The Cummings traveled back and forth between New York and California with regularity during the 1920s. Victor Cumming was visiting Dorothy in California when he died in 1926. In any case, it is likely that Kahn's visit to *The King of Kings* lot led to Rose's acquaintance with him.

That the acquaintance with Rose did develop—and blossom—is certain because it is received wisdom, common knowledge—call it what you will—that Rose became the mistress of Otto Kahn. Mark Hampton says in *Legendary Decorators of the Twentieth Century*:

Rose Cumming … is especially fascinating because she was, in addition to being a marvelous decorator, a colorful character and a great courtesan, the mistress of a titanically rich financier whose largesse kept her in business long after she quit decorating. Her enchanting shop, thanks to this terrific endowment, went on for years and years with practically no real business being conducted in it.

Rose's sister Eileen, as late as 1979, 11 years after Rose's death, wrote a reproachful letter to the *New York Times*, calling the story of Rose's liaison a "canard." The Times had printed an article about legendary decorators in which it said that she was the mistress of Otto Kahn. Eileen wrote that the story sprang from Rose having lush displays of fruit and flowers on her desk in the shop, which she said came from "the Kahn greenhouses." Eileen claimed that Rose had just done a little decorating work for Mrs. Kahn who sent the fruit and floral offerings. But the story of Rose and Otto lived, and continues to live.

Russell Cecil, Eileen's son, and his wife, Nancy, say they do not know whether the Kahn story is true or not. Susan Loney, however, an interior designer who is Rose's great-niece by her half-sister, Margery Loney, who lived with Rose in old age, says categorically that the story is true.

Certainly, in the early 1930s, when Rose was in terrible financial trouble, someone gave her the lease of the shop at 515 Madison Avenue, where she stayed for nearly 30 years,

May 31, 1979

HOW DO RUMORS START ?--
PARTICULARLY LIBELOUS ONES

On Thursday, May 31st, an article appeared in the New York
Times entitled, GRANDES DAMES OF DECORATING'S EARLY YEARS
which included the much admired and sometimes maligned
Rose Cumming.

It carries two unfortunate and untrue statements:
1) "the beautiful Rose Cumming, reputedly the mistress of
    Otto Kahn, the financier..... and
2) "given to wearing chiffon over her nakedness...."

Rose Cumming never even met Mr. Kahn but she was fortunate
in having Mrs. Kahn as a client; nothing prodigious but
helping to refurbish her very beautiful New York house.
Mrs. Kahn liked and admired Miss Cumming's work and enjoyed
coming to the shop to discuss the work in progress and she
nearly always came bearing gifts of rare flowers or fruit
from her greenhouses. Miss Cumming loved these offerings
and they would be displayed on her desk and much admired.
In answer to the many queries as to where she found such
perfection out of season she would say proudly,"they came
from the Kahn greenhouses." Enter here the beginnings of
the canard.

The second remark is also most unfortunate, "chiffon over
her nakedness"-- was, of course, not true but it does give
a picture of a very different person from one who wore her
famous decolletage with a bit of daring and a lot of beauty!

ABOVE An article in the May 31, 1979, *New York Times* entitled
"Grandes Dames of Decorating's Early Years" mentioned Rose
Cumming as "reputedly the mistress of Otto Kahn" who was "given
to wearing chiffon over her nakedness." Eileen Cecil, guardian of
the family's reputation, had her granddaughter, Sarah, type out this
furious rebuttal to the paper. *Dessin Fournir Collections.*

for little or no rent. Otto Kahn died in 1934, but the lease may have been in perpetuity. Even Eileen admits that Rose had the space for very little rent, attributing the fact to the building's wanting to have design world tenants. Everyone in the design world today, however, particularly elder statesmen such as Mario Buatta, William Hodgins—who worked for Rose—Thomas Britt, and Albert Hadley concur that Rose had a liaison with Otto Kahn.

With Rose's adventuresome past, a liaison would not seem shocking to her, and she always went for the titles and big names—counts, barons, and, one suspects, "the King of New York."

Dorothy's career in the movies came to an abrupt halt in 1929 with the advent of the talkies. Among her last films were *The Wind*, starring Lillian Gish and directed by Victor Sjostrom, which was one of the last silent films released by Metro-Goldwyn-Mayer, and *Our Dancing Daughters*, starring Joan Crawford. But the acting years had been lucrative and Dorothy's connections important contacts for Rose. In Rose's address book, which was taken over by Eileen at her death, there are addresses and phone numbers for Marlene Dietrich, Gloria Swanson, Norma Shearer, and Mary Pickford. Certainly these people all came into the shop when they were in New York. It is unclear just how much decorating work Rose did in California for the movie stars, but she certainly would have known some of them. The interior of a house belonging to Marlene Dietrich has Rose's signature touches of silver paper on the walls and jewel-tone upholstery, and Bungalow No. 7 at the Beverly Hills Hotel, which Marlene Dietrich called "her" bungalow, used Rose's chintz fabric, "Garden of Allah." A beach house at Malibu shared by Norma Shearer and her husband, Irving Thalberg—the director genius who died young and who was the model for Monroe Stahr, the hero of F. Scott Fitzgerald's Hollywood novel *The Last Tycoon*—also has touches of Rose's style such as Venetian mirrors and heavy satin draperies.

Anthony Cumming, Dorothy's surviving son, says, "When we came back to New York in 1929, we moved to Southampton." Dorothy, with her movie earnings, bought—or perhaps Rose, who was working a lot at the time, bought with her—an eighteenth-century shingled, Cape Cod–style cottage in Southampton village. This house gave Rose great print exposure.

There are two articles about the Southampton cottage, one in *House & Garden* in July 1930 and one in *Arts & Decoration* some years later. The *House & Garden* article identifies the owner of the house as Dorothy (Mrs. Cumming Elliott, a name created after her divorce) and Rose as the decorator. The later article names Rose as the the cottage's owner.

Rose's nephew, Russell Cecil, who remembers both the cottage and his aunt fondly, the latter with a justified dash of cynicism, says, "The cottage was eighteenth century, so of course Rose had to say that it was seventeenth century."

The caption in *Arts & Decoration* for the picture of the exterior, with its charming picket fence says, "Miss Cumming's little old shingle house on Long Island dates back to 1660, and has a romantic history of many centuries. It is practically unchanged today—just made convenient and livable." The story is continued in the second and longer article for which Rose told the writer that the cottage was built in 1660 by a baker and his wife who immigrated to Southampton from England. While Southampton was the first English settlement in New York, founded in 1640 by Puritan settlers from Massachusetts, Dorothy and Rose's cottage, with its relatively large windows is distinctly eighteenth century.

The interior of the cottage is done in an elegant country style, furnished with English antiques and knickknacks that Rose had picked up abroad and which stocked her shop.

*[W]hen Miss Cumming furnished her cottage she had the choice of pieces which the baker and his wife had never heard of. New Yorkers have passed Miss Cumming's shop on Madison Avenue often enough and seen the fantastic display of fine objects and chintz and wall-paper and furniture and bibelots of every period. Miss Cumming had only to make an appropriate choice from all this richness to furnish her cottage in Southampton. When the baker arrived from England, Queen Anne had not been heard of, much less the style in furniture that was typical of her reign. But Miss Cumming chose that style, nevertheless, as suitable to her house in Southampton. (*Arts & Decoration, *March 1937)*

The antiques in the living room are set against a background of Rose's characteristic jewel tones and gleaming surfaces. The ceiling and walls are papered in lacquer green. The window curtains are framed in scalloped cornices and side panels of stiffened yellow chintz with apple-green piping. There is an old Samarkand rug in violet and jade green on the floor. In the corner is a Lancashire gateleg table; and there is a Queen Anne desk and lowboy with spindle-backed Jacobean chairs placed around the room. In a juxtaposition very characteristic of Rose's taste for mingling unlikely pieces in order to highlight each, a gilt-framed Queen Anne mirror over the fireplace looks down on a primitive Old English milking stool squatting on the hearth.

The dining room has a Welsh cupboard that displays some of Rose's valuable Staffordshire china in a mauve-and-plum colored pattern. Upstairs the bedrooms are open under the eaves with heavy, hand-hewn eighteenth-century beams crossing the room. The bedroom upholstery is peach, orange, and yellow satin mixed with Old English flowered chintz at the windows, again showing Rose's daring and completely successful mix of the smart and the homely.

RIGHT The Southampton cottage that Dorothy bought in 1929, when she gave up her Hollywood career and came back east. It was decorated by Rose. *Southampton Historical Museum.*

Rose furnished the living room of the cottage with an antique English milking stool and miniature chair and lots of chintz including this woodblock print chintz labeled #249 from Rose's archives. *Courtesy of Sarah Cumming Cecil.*

Rose had an eighteenth-century cottage in Southampton. Everybody loved it. Its name was "Green Shutters," and you could go to the pharmacy in Southampton where they had all the postcards and there were postcards of "Green Shutters." This house absolutely knocked your eyes out. The characteristic ceiling height of a farmhouse of that period was 6' 8". Rose and Dorothy took down the ceilings upstairs and exposed the beams to show the slope of the roof. All the rooms were marvelous and the continuity of it was marvelous.

Russell Cecil, architect and Rose Cumming's nephew

Rose opened the ceiling to the hand-hewn beams on the second floor and placed a Welsh cupboard in the dining room. She boldly dressed up the rustic interior with gleaming jewel tones, such as the peach satin bed cover. *Arts & Decoration,* May 1937. *Art & Architecture Collection, Miriam and Ira D. Wallach Division of Art, Prints and Photographs, the New York Public Library, Astor, Lenox and Tilden Foundations.*

[In Rose's house on Fifty-third Street] every surface was reflective. The paints, as I recall were all high gloss enamel…and the rooms glistened. And then floors were polished within an inch of their lives…and so you were in these townhouse sized rooms and they just went from one to the other and the experience changed drastically as these colors changed.

Russell Cecil,
architect and nephew of Rose Cumming

OPPOSITE Rose frequently set mirrors into walls to seemingly expand the space and create mystery. The two pagodas were her possessions, so this may be an early view of her house on West Fifty-third Street.
Dessin Fournir Collections.

CHAPTER SIX

The 1930s:
Shining Surfaces and Trouble Underneath

Earlier in her career, in the 1920s, Rose's decorating tended to be traditional in theme, although, with her eccentric eye, there were always unexpected small touches, such as faience cats. In fact, Rose wrote an article for the December 1927 *House & Garden* called "Faience Cats in Decoration."

Chinese craftsmen frequently turned their genius to the moulding of queer, long-eared cats; both the Chelsea and Staffordshire factories made many delightful cat studies, and Garfee, of Nancy, is responsible for some of the most charming old faience cats we have. It is amazing what variety of expression these little models have—pride, anger, coyness, disdain, desire, contentment—all are portrayed in clay, and when placed "right" they introduce an amusing and homely note into the most formal decorative scheme.

Rose's bringing to life her faience cats is typical of the love she bore for her treasures. Her sister Eileen remembers Rose saying many times, "These beautiful things are my children." Nonetheless, Rose's early work has a sobering preponderance of imposing eighteenth-century portraits and grand eighteenth-century secretary desks. Although in her own home, her irrepressible sense of color asserted itself with the red japanned secretary in her library.

By the early 1930s, however, Rose had discovered silver-leaf paper for the walls and ceiling and silver lamé—and even on occasion cellophane—for draperies. The 1930s was the decade of shiny surfaces: there were Art Deco chrome decorations on automobiles and aluminum coffee services and satin dresses that clung to Jean Harlow. There was a fascination with new synthetic fabrics. Cole

Miss Cumming's Bedroom

Walls
Mauve Bedford

Curtains Janof 17798

- Sofa

Walls
Silver Panels by Avinoff

Curtains

Gold Lame

Glass Curtains

Miss Cumming's Bathroom

Walls   Cur

Slipper
Bergere Chair   Floor #47 E4

Porter's "You're the Top" carols "…you're the lovely light of a summer night in Spain / You're the National Gallery, you're Garbo's salary, you're cellophane!" Rose adopted the new technology with enthusiasm, and she had no problem combining it with her antiques. She was fearless. Mark Hampton in *Legendary Decorators of the Twentieth Century* describes her bedroom as having "walls covered in shiny metallic, midnight-blue paper, the kind on the box of a bottle of Evening in Paris perfume."

Rose's use of silver leaf paper brings up points of comparison between her work and that of two of her contemporaries, Syrie Maugham and Dorothy Draper. Although Rose was unique, she was part of the same aesthetic and cultural climate of Art Deco with classical roots that allowed these two talented women to flourish, and it is worth looking at points where they all crossed.

Syrie Maugham was married between 1913 and 1929 to Somerset Maugham, the famous novelist, playwright, and short-story writer, whose work is somewhat derided these days for being "middle brow," but who could tell a story as well as anyone who ever wrote. Maugham was homosexual and the marriage was stormy—despite the fact that Syrie loved him and loved that he was one of the most famous writers of his generation.

In 1921, Syrie opened a shop in London—the same year that Rose opened her shop in New York—and like Rose's shop, Syrie's functioned in the European way of selling antiques, fabrics, and furniture, and Syrie's services as a decorator. Syrie became famous in the decorating world for her all-white rooms, although, as Mark Hampton points out, "it was not just the all white room that interested her." She liked soft colors, but, says Hampton, she also:

loved rock crystal and mirrors, often covering bathroom walls and screens and furniture itself with mirrors, as other people were doing at the time; however, she did it in a particularly rich way that was refined rather than appearing like something out of the ladies' room in a nightclub. She was devoted to satin and shiny surfaces.

Hampton, in fact, says, when describing Rose's bedroom, "the curtains were silver gauze, hanging from mirrored

OPPOSITE Rose's use of metallic silver leaf on the walls of a bedroom was a particularly 1930s motif shared by her fellow decorator Syrie Maugham, but Rose did it with more panache. *Collection of the New-York Historical Society, Matte E. Hewitt and Richard A. Smith Collection.*

109

pelmets in a twenties design that recalled Syrie Maugham." He also says that Syrie Maugham "was known at the time to like Regency furniture when other people considered it not serious enough to be valued." While Syrie championed Regency furniture, Rose was an early advocate of the nearly contemporaneous French Directoire.

Rose and Syrie Maugham knew each other; Syrie worked in the United States—even having a shop in New York at one point—and Rose traveled to London. Sarah Cecil, Rose's great-niece, says that when Syrie closed her New York shop someone proposed to Rose that she make white furniture, but she replied, "No, white is for Syrie." It is not likely that there was any direct influence between the two women, but it is interesting that two of the most original decorators of the period shared tastes for satin and shiny walls of silver leaf and mirrors and delicate early nineteenth-century furniture.

The other decorator of the period whose work bears a comparison with Rose's was Dorothy Draper. Larger than life in her person and her projects—she towered over her male businessmen clients, boasting the imposing bosom of a Helen Hokinson cartoon character, and she worked mostly on big hotels—Dorothy Draper also broke the mold. One of her first commissions was the new Carlyle Hotel on Madison Avenue in the late 1920s. Mark Hampton says "the decoration of the Carlyle lobby pointed in the direction her style would follow for the next thirty years: crisply geometric marble floors in black, grey, and white, immaculate white plaster and lush, tufted furniture with a touch of Belle Epoque opulence."

The mixture of the Belle Epoque furniture and classical embellishments with a bold black and white Art Deco color scheme was a decorating approach that Rose would have acknowledged, although her own work was more complicated and fantastical.

Confirmation that Dorothy Draper and Rose knew each other—and that also shows the comfortable overlapping of services in the design world in those days—was the fact that Dorothy was a client of Rose's, buying antiques in her shop. Mark Hampton says of the Carlyle lobby, "Only the antique tapestries from Rose Cumming's shop…fell into the traditional vocabulary of hotel-lobby decoration."

Rose used silver leaf on the walls and ceiling with a particularly happy result in the dining room of her sister Eileen Cecil's house on East Fifty-eighth Street. Rose would use Eileen's house as a sort of template for trying out new ideas over the years, and this scheme was successful enough to have a painting done of it, which was reproduced in an issue of *House & Garden* in the 1930s. The glazing and the colors are classic Rose. The caption states:

The New York City dining room of Eileen and Russell LaFayette Cecil, decorated by Mrs. Cecil's sister Rose Cumming … Silver-leafed walls glazed with periwinkle blue, silver tea paper ceiling, plum-colored carpet, midnight-blue draperies with pink curtains, overmantel painting-on-mirror by Robert Pichenot and Dart Thorne, and bowl shaped vase with flowering branches of dogwood. Watercolor by David Payne for House & Garden.

The year 1932 was a watershed for the Cumming family. In the society pages of the *New York Times* for August 3, 1932, there was the following item:

Mrs. Victor Cumming of 400 East Fifty-seventh Street announces the marriage of her daughter, Mrs. Dorothy Cumming Elliott, former stage and screen actress, to Allan McNab, British artist, last Wednesday. The ceremony was performed by the Reverend Dr. Edward Henry Emett, pastor of the Manhattan Congregational Church, in the presence of relatives and close friends at Mrs. Cumming's apartment.

The bride's last appearance on Broadway was when she played Naomi in "Judas" in January 1929.

Allan McNab was a British graphic designer as well as an artist. He became the art director of *Life* magazine, worked as a design director for film director Norman Bel Geddes, and became director of administration of the Art Institute of Chicago. For several years after Dorothy married him they lived in England and Dorothy's sons went back and forth between the United States and England.

Two and a half months later a cataclysmic event for Rose took place. On the premises of the Anderson Gallery at Park Avenue and Fifty-ninth Street, where Rose had had her shop and studio for almost ten years, a three-day auction took place at which almost her entire inventory of antiques and wallpapers was sold off.

OPPOSITE Rose echoed the flora painted on the walls of this bathroom in the live flowers blooming in the built-in planter around the tub. *Library of Congress, Arnold Genthe Collection.*

Eileen Cecil's New York living room, decorated by Rose, was embellished with her signature coromandel screens, mirrors and crystal chandeliers.
Photograph by Wendy Hilty.

Rose's design scheme for "Mrs. Cecil's bath" shown with the original woodblock print found in her archives. Named "La Vigne Chinoise," this fabric is being reintroduced to the collection.
Photograph by Jayson K. T. Schwaller,
Dessin Fournir Collections.

Although the reason given for the sale was litigation between the owner and the lessor of the Anderson Gallery, from whom Rose had a sublease, thereby necessitating that Rose find a new—and smaller—space for a shop, it is almost certainly true that Rose had lost most of her clientele in the deepening Depression and had to sell her inventory to survive.

"The Depression almost smashed Rose up," said Eileen in later years.

Thirteen million people were unemployed in the United States between 1929 and the U.S. entry into World War II in 1941. At the worst of the Depression, in 1932–33, people in families with no regular wage earner totaled 34 million. Home building dropped by 80 percent and the income of the average American family was reduced by 40 percent between 1929 and 1932. Even in the rarified world of Rose's clients, there were drastic consequences: corporate profits dropped from ten billion dollars in 1929 to one billion in 1932.

Rose's auction at the Anderson Galleries was a huge event. The 131-page catalogue lists 605 lots spread out over three afternoons. The foreword to the catalogue, written by the Plaza Art Auction Galleries, who were handling the sale, describe Rose's character and style as they would be known for the rest of her life:

The Rose Cumming Galleries have been a landmark of New York, situated in one of the most central cross roads of the Metropolis. Her bold signature wrought in bronze, and adorning the front of the old Anderson Galleries building has been indicative of her originality and daring. Both in her selection of distinguished and rare art objects and in the subtle combination of colour values in her handling of textiles, Miss Cumming has had few equals among the leading decorative artists and collectors in this country. She has been particularly successful in the introduction of Chinese paper wall covering as background for well-bred and imaginative drawing rooms. She has also excelled in the design of table glass and her goblets and rummers, which are included in this sale, with encrusted figurines representing hunts have an explicable charm on the dining table.

The furniture chosen by Miss Cumming has always had a consistent quality. She refused to acquire the commonplace and the examples in her collection representing Georgian England and France of the Louis' as well as the exceptionally fine collection of Regency pieces, show a deep understanding of the cabinet maker's art. This point is most strikingly illustrated by examination of such examples as the large drum table, the rare lectern tables, and the superb extension dining tables and sideboards.

Among the lots—in addition to the star piece of the eighteenth-century English room in carved pine paneling questionably attributed to William Kent noted earlier—there was enormous variety. There were dining tables and chairs, mugs, vases, and clocks. A "Harpsichord X-Stool of the Consulate" is listed on a page facing a carved piecrust tilt-top table ("English, XVIII Century"). There are pages of screens—an eight-fold coromandel along with "The Richmond Paper," which is "Twelve Panels of 'Duke of Richmond.' Panels of Magnificent Painted Paper Wainscot with Flowers and Birds in the Chinese European Taste of 1700." The collection ranges from Cararra marble fireplace surrounds to a "Set of six glass table ornaments of contemporary English workmanship; four red-coats on galloping mounts, an unmounted horse, and pair of hounds, the gaily colored figurines incrusted in globes."

Sometimes the implied attributions and provenances almost outweigh the descriptions. A good number of pieces come from the collection of Rose's friend Millicent, Duchess of Sutherland; and a "Rolled Top High Secretaire of the Hepplewhite Period" is "From the Lord Leverhulme Collection."

The sale seems to have done quite well. An article in the *New York Times* for Friday morning, October 28, the second day of the sale, reports sales at the first session brought $6,367, $105,400 in early twenty-first century currency, with two big days still to come.

Following the auction, Rose the remaining baggage and moved to 515 Madison Avenue at the corner of Madison and East Fifty-third Street, just a short block and a half from her house on West Fifty-third Street, where she would remain for the next 30 years.

515 Madison had opened in 1931. It was designed by J. E. R. Carpenter who was paired in popularity with the now fairly well-known Rosario Candela as the architect of most of the luxury apartment houses built on Fifth Avenue between the wars. Carpenter designed altogether nearly 125 buildings along Fifth, Park, and Madison avenues. It was said that Carpenter and his family moved in the same circles as the residents of his luxury buildings and that he was frequently mentioned in the society columns. Sadly Carpenter died in 1932, one year after 515 Madison was completed and the year of Rose's auction. Carpenter died insolvent. At his death, he left an estate of $149,000 and debts of $911,000.

Certainly someone gave Rose an extremely sweet deal on the 515 Madison Avenue shop space. There were interior designers' offices and fabric and antique companies across the street, and they were eager to promote the area as a nascent design center. How that may have played into Rose's sweetheart deal is not known, but even her sister Eileen, who was a model of rectitude and the guardian of the family reputation admitted, as we have said, that Rose was practically welcomed to the place for free. It is not clear who backed the building financially, but Otto Kahn, among his many interests, invested in real estate ; and with Mr. Carpenter being a well-known figure socially along upper Fifth Avenue, as was Mr. Kahn (he walked his dachshunds along the avenue daily when he was in town), it seems not too much of a stretch to subscribe to the legend that Otto Kahn was the benefactor for Rose's shop.

Rose was intensely concerned with image—the beautiful images of her antiques and the rooms she decorated, the images reflected in her polished floors and the mirrors she loved, and the image she herself presented to the world physically and as a personality. Two photographs of her remain that were taken in her prime during the early 1930s, just before her clearinghouse auction, after which she settled into the shop at 515 Madison and became a character—and a sibyl to the design world.

The two iconic photographs show her as beautiful, glamorous, thoughtful and warm—just as she wanted to be perceived. The first was taken by Edward Steichen, the photo-secessionist photographer who was famous during the first half of the twentieth century in the art and photography worlds, and who was the in-house photographer for Condé Nast through the 1920s and 1930s. Steichen's portrait of Greta Garbo, taken in 1928, is widely credited with helping her along in her American career.

Steichen's portrait of Rose shows her elaborately dressed in a velvet brocade gown (with a low décolletage, of course). She is sitting on an antique sofa with a cachepot filled with flowers on a pedestal behind her and a gilt framed mirror above her—all the emblems of her trade. On her nimbus of gray hair there is a small wreath of flowers. The dark brows contrasting with her hair are serious, and she wears a slight pensive smile. The photograph is in effect an advertisement. "Look at how sensitive I am and what good taste I have," it says. "I will make your life perfect." It is the photograph of a courtesan who is selling a way of life rather than sex. We have said that Rose's social life and personal life were conducted as means of selling people her vision of beauty and, not incidentally, her designs and her antiques. The Steichen portrait perfectly captures this.

The other portrait is a sort of formal snapshot by Arnold Genthe. Genthe had emigrated from Germany in 1895 to San Francisco, where he taught himself photography. He is well known for his photographs of San Francisco's Chinatown taken before the earthquake of 1906, and best known for his photographs of the earthquake itself. In 1911, he moved to New York where he became primarily a portraitist of the famous, including Theodore Roosevelt, Woodrow Wilson, and John D. Rockefeller, as well as the celebrated dancers Anna Pavlova and Isadora Duncan. Genthe's 1925 portrait of Garbo, predating Steichen's, is thought to have opened the door to her American career.

Rose, with her instinct for people with connections who could help her career, hired (or more likely persuaded) Arnold Genthe to take a series of photographs of rooms she had designed in the late 1920s. The rooms are mostly in her grand style, made distinctive by her favorite Chinese

RIGHT Rose deeply loved her family, which, along with her passion for antiques, was the constant in her life. In the late 1920s, she cajoled society photographer Arnold Genthe to take an informal portrait in Newport of her mother, to her left, her perennial escort, Count Antonio Algaro, standing behind Sarah Cumming, and her little nephew, Russell Cecil, whose leg Rose protectively holds. *Photograph by Arnold Genthe, courtesy of Sarah Cumming Cecil.*

wallpaper and unexpected groupings of furniture, although there is one photograph of a bathroom paneled in mirrors with hand-painted flower decoration that combines chinoiserie and Art Deco. To sweeten the deal for Genthe, however—and how much sweetening was involved we will never know—Rose invited him to Newport, the high-society resort in Rhode Island, where she had a house for several summers. (In fact, with her characteristic desire to belong and bravura that simultaneously tarnished her social credentials, Rose was once asked to leave Bailey's Beach, the ultraexclusive beach club in Newport, because her bathing costume was too skimpy.)

Genthe took candid portraits of Sarah Fennell Cumming, Rose's statuesque mother, walking on the lawn. The loyalty of the sisters to each other and their devotion to their parents was one of the most genuine things about them, and a group portrait by Genthe is a touching testimony to Rose's human side. As long as her mother lived, Rose included her in her life—even calling one of the rooms in her Xanadu-like house on Fifty-third Street "Mother's room." The Genthe photograph shows Rose and her mother in Newport, Rose wearing a large-brimmed 1920s hat that shades her eyes, both women sitting on a Victorian iron garden bench. Behind Mrs. Cumming stands the darkly handsome Antonio Algara, one of Rose's permanent escorts, and on the other side a laughing man helps four-year-old Russell Cecil Jr. stand on a table. Rose's one arm is stretched out to support Russell's leg; the other is behind her mother's shoulder. It was Newport, Rose is smartly dressed, Antonio Algaro is exotic and sleek, but it is her mother and nephew whom she holds onto.

OPPOSITE Rose, photographed in the late 1920s by Edward Steichen, who was the official photographer for Condé Nast from 1923 to 1938. A photograph such as this, appearing in *Vogue*, put the seal on Rose's position as symbol of style and arbiter of taste. *Photograph by Edward Steichen, Dessin Fournir Collections.*

*She revitalized tired things by re-coloring them.
Familiar chintzes, shy linens were dyed in fresh
tones—pinks, oranges with red, lavenders
with purples and blues—incredible in the
conservative '20s and '30s.*

Eleanor Spaak, journalist

CHAPTER SEVEN

Settling In

After the Anderson Gallery sale in 1932, when Rose was settled in her smaller, but more distinctive, shop at 515 Madison Avenue, she began seriously to add contemporary fabrics to her inventory of antiques and antique brocades and velvets. The fabrics, one of the principal creative acts for which she is remembered, were mostly chintzes. They provided a consistent source of income over the decades, as well as a means of expression for her talent with color. Mark Hampton noted that

Rose had great success during her career with her boldly colored chintzes, but the colors were nothing like the bold colors of our time. No shocking pink, poison green, or buttercup yellow. They were rather the colors of flowers in a Winterhalter painting ... Where Rose was superior to most others in the field of decorating was as a colorist, the facet of her talent that enabled her to produce the beautiful chintzes that carry her name to this day. She used sapphire blue, mauve, purple, heliotrope, and orchid colors in a way that no one else would have dared attempt.

The fabrics are her tangible legacy, just as the influence she had on young designers, who would become leaders in the field, is her intangible legacy.

The chintzes that Rose is known for are the generic results of a long line of fabric production that had begun in India in the seventeenth century. The word *chintz* is thought to have come from the Hindu word *cheita* or Sanskrit *citra*, both of which mean "spotted," "variegated," or "colored." Chintz was originally a calico, a cotton fabric with a bold

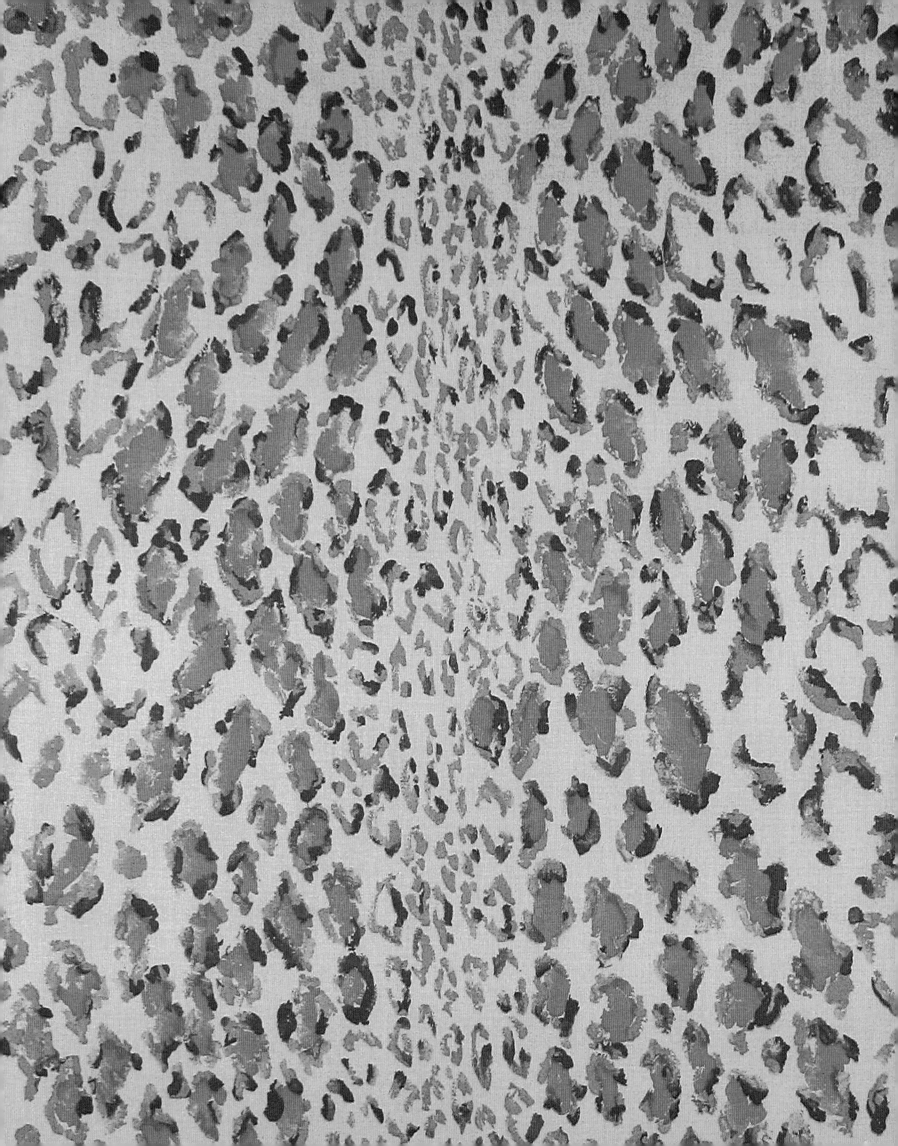

Original document of Rose Cumming "Royal Swag."
Photograph by Jayson K. T. Schwaller, Dessin Fournir Collections.

design of flowers and animals, hand printed with woodblocks or painted or stained. The fabric was usually glazed with wax or starch.

Indian chintzes were first brought to Europe around 1600. They were used for bedcovers, clothing, and draperies. Even though they were rare and expensive, chintzes were so popular that wool and silk mills in both France and England felt threatened. In 1686, France declared a ban on chintz imports, and England did the same in 1722. By the middle of the eighteenth century, however, French and English mills had acquired the skills of printing with carved wooden hand blocks, and the bans were repealed.

In the middle of the nineteenth century, the term *chintz* usually meant glazed cotton fabric printed with large designs of flowers, leaves, and flowering branches. (Unglazed cotton prints were often called cretonne; these were popular in designs created by William Morris for the Arts and Crafts movement of the late nineteenth century.) By about 1900, glazed chintz was again popular for draperies and upholstery.

In England, chintz was used primarily in country houses (thus becoming the signature for what became known in the late twentieth century in the American decorating world as the "English Country House Look"), and, similarly, in the early part of the twentieth century in America chintz was considered to be informal and suitable mostly for the country. Along with her pioneering use of chintz, Rose Cumming and her fabrics were significantly responsible for bringing chintz into the drawing room.

Probably starting in the 1920s, but certainly in the 1930s, Rose regularly visited fabric vendors and their mills in England and France on her annual trips to Europe (which lasted until World War II and were resumed again in the 1950s). The firms tended to be long established ones. One firm in England had been founded in 1891; there was a mill in the north of England that was known for the unique vibrancy of the colors it produced, which was attributed to the local water that was used in the dying process. A mill in the Loire Valley in France had been founded in 1829. Rose would take her sketches to the vendors, sometimes drawing on different

elements of designs from their archives, and work with the mills mixing colors until she had created designs with the mauves, heliotropes, lavenders, and salmons that were uniquely her palette.

Among the first of her designs was "Chestnut Leaves," a pattern of full leaves in different shades of green on a cream background. It is striking in the variations of green it presents. In Mark Hampton's *Legendary Decorators* book, he has painted a watercolor of a Long Island sunroom decorated by Elsie Cobb Wilson that shows "Chestnut Leaves" on a sofa and two Louis XV–style chairs.

"Eileen," named for Rose's sister, has bouquets of multi-colored flowers; originally on a white background, still available it also comes on blue, pink, and taupe. "Calla Lilies," a dramatic, trumpet-shaped flower popular in the 1930s, has the lilies printed life size with leaves in shades of green on a resounding black background; it is also available on burgundy and taupe.

Two fabrics that have decorative elements included in them are "Lace" and "Cumming Rose." "Lace" shows swags of lace sketched onto a background of Rose's favorite salmon color with small bouquets at the knots of the lace; it is also available on pink and mauve. "Cumming Rose" has large bows and streamers of ribbon surrounding bunches of roses—with the thorns showing incidentally. Printed in France, the original background color was pink; it is now available on robin's egg blue, taupe, and camel.

Perhaps the best known of Rose's chintzes is "Delphinium." It incorporates Rose's signature colors of grape, several shades of lilac, mauve, and orchid. Originally printed on a background of black stripes on taupe, the tall stalks of delphinium with their blending colors now lean toward each other across a white background. The colors echoed the in jewel tones that bedecked the guest room in her house. Mark Hampton says: "In the middle of the house was what Rose always referred to as her mother's room, decorated in shades of lilac and mauve and her famous delphinium chintz. In the center of the room stood a beautiful French bed draped in swagged and pleated orchid-colored taffeta."

"Carisbrook" was an early chintz that had its popularity proven many, many years after Rose had introduced it to New York. It is an overscale print of flowers in red and yellow and a metallic gray-green on a dusty-rose background. (It is also available on a chartreuse background.) Michael Taylor, the renowned California decorator, known for his overscale "California Look," came into the shop when it was on East Fifty-ninth Street, a number of years after Rose's death; Eileen Cecil and her business partner, Ronald Grimaldi, were running a somewhat skeleton operation at that point. Michael Taylor insisted that he had to have 70 yards of "Carisbrook." There were eight or ten yards in the shop. The mill in England would only print 70 yards if two other fabrics in a comparable volume were ordered as well. Eileen and Ron took deep breaths and ordered 70 yards each of "Carisbrook," "Cumming Rose," and "Delphinium." They sold—and soon—and the business was up and running again.

New York designer Thomas Britt, a close friend of Rose's when he was a young man, says about her fabrics, "There was nothing like them for scale and color. She had a ravishing, glorious, sophisticated sense of color. In a way, she took chintzes back to what they had been when they first came from India and China in the seventeenth and eighteenth centuries and adapted them to her own aesthetic. She—and the chintzes—were unique."

Similarly, the elder statesman of design Albert Hadley says, "Miss Rose's palette and her interesting aesthetics made her fabrics unique in the trade."

Both of these accomplished designers, who have been at the top of their profession for decades, also mention several fabrics developed by Rose's sister Dorothy that are very different from the line of chintzes created by Rose. "Banana Leaves" is a huge design of banana leaves printed almost in the abstract form of a photographic negative. Albert Hadley noted they had used it when he worked at McMillen in the late 1950s. Today it is available on white with the leaves in either a bright green or gold.

RIGHT Original document of Rose Cumming "Carisbrook." *Photograph by Jayson K. T. Schwaller, Dessin Fournir Collections.*

Two other fabrics created by Dorothy with a similar primitive quality include "Metallic Bird," an abstract pattern in gold on rust or green or yellow, and "Santa Fe," a geometric pattern, almost folk art, of diamond shapes inside an eight-pointed star inside an image of swirling lines. The latter comes on white with the diamond pattern and the eight-pointed star in rust or green or yellow.

Dorothy's son, Anthony Cumming, explains how these came about:

Regarding the "Banana Leaves"...My mother[,] Dorothy Cumming[,] moved to Jamaica after her divorce from Allan McNab and needed something to do. She had made material using blocks (which I made) when in New York using some kind of gold looking paint and asked Aunt Rose to sell them for her. Which she did and they were quite popular. In Jamaica she had no blocks as I was off elsewhere[,] so she tried banana leaves straight off of the hillside, also other kinds of leaves. She made them into materials which hotels used to decorate rooms with curtains, bedspreads etc. As they were popular in Jamaica she asked Aunt Rose to sell them in New York. Which she did and marketed a lot of yardage. Aunt Rose's great chintzes and fabrics were complemented by the primitive yardage[,] [although Rose's fabrics were] far superior of course. The McNab leaf material sold there and in Jamaica at Dorothy McNab stores in Montego Bay, Ocho Rios[,] and hotels such as Round Hill, Bay Roc, Half Moon etc...

The gist of what I am saying is that Aunt Rose was as usual helping my mother by selling her stuff for her in N.Y.[,] but had no direct other manufacturing involvement. Rose was always helping others and of course her sisters.

There are stories, created by the legend that Rose embodied in her own person, of her high-handed ways of dealing with customers who displeased her. One day, a demanding woman kept saying she couldn't see the fabric well enough in the light of the shop to know whether she wanted to buy it. In exasperation, Rose took the bolt of fabric onto Madison Avenue and, disregarding traffic, rolled it out across the street. "There!" she said, "Can you see it well enough now? It doesn't matter in any case, because it's no longer for sale."

OPPOSITE "Banana Leaves" is the fabric that Dorothy Cumming created in Jamaica by hacking leaves off a banana tree, dipping them in paint and pressing them onto cloth. She sent the fabric to Rose to sell, and it became iconic in Rose's line. *Photograph by Jayson K. T. Schwaller, Dessin Fournir Collections.*

Original handblock print called "Hart & Bird" from Rose's
collection used on the bench in her front hall.
Photograph by Jayson K. T. Schwaller, Dessin Fournir Collections.

Rose's front hall with an eighteenth-century English aviary that the catalogue for her 1951 house tour called "pre-Chippendale" and described as "perhaps the most enchanting birdhouse in America."
Photograph by Harold Haliday Costain, Dessin Fournir Collections.

A good sense of the appeal of Rose's shop and personality—and the mixture that it all was—comes through in a letter written to her in her old age by a man who signed it "Michael O'S."

Dear Miss Rosy-Posy….

I've often thought about what a genuinely triumphant person you are. In all the years I've passed by your window, and known you, I have never ever seen a single object in your possession that wasn't beautiful, that I wouldn't love to have. And your fabulous ability to toss and flipflap things about making them all land in endless "Still Lifes" that would beguile any artist. Just the way you dump a mile of mauve satin into your window, or plump a Chinese frog into a Venetian chair, or turn Pauline Borghese's bed into a pool of flowers (how Freud would have appreciated that too!)—I did love your flower shop with its Fifty-third Street Niagara…Over the years there has never been a let down. You might be surprised to know how often, in the old days, when life seemed too full of disappointments, when I was terribly depressed, and even hungry, I would pull myself together and go and see what Rosy-Posy had in her windows—sometimes in the middle of the night—and always it would be refreshing, and manage to renew my faith in the skies overhead…So you see, dear Rose, how profoundly indebted I am to you for so much…

Through the 1930s, Rose's social life continued to whirl, even as the Depression took a toll on her business. On October 1, 1932, just before the Anderson Gallery auction, she was listed in the society columns of the *New York Times* at a dinner given by Mr. and Mrs. Victor White in the Starlight roof garden of the Waldorf-Astoria. In 1935, the society columns noted that Rose and her frequent escort Antonio Algara attended a dinner given by Colonel Charles E. Greenough for Colonel Sir William Acland and Lady Acland at La Maisonette Russe of the St. Regis. And on August 24, 1936, under a general heading "Many Entertain At Southampton," the Times recorded that "Miss Rose Cumming gave an informal reception this afternoon at her home for Frederick Hughes who arrived recently from Australia for a visit." Frederick

Hughes was the half brother of Rose, Eileen, and Dorothy from Mrs. Cumming's first marriage.

Rose seems to have enjoyed a certain raffish seasoning in her social life. According to Julie Britt, the former wife of Thomas Britt and also a friend of Rose's in her old age, Rose would go to tea dances at the Waldorf-Astoria in the 1930s, chaperoned by her mother, and dance with Ted Peckham, the male dance partner for hire on staff there. A reproduction of a Los Angeles *Herald-Examiner* photograph of Peckham from April 28, 1937, has the caption: "Ted Peckham…who ran an L.A. outfit called 'Super Gigolo Service,' shows 'the elite way' for a male escort to light a woman's cigarette."

Julie remembers that when Rose was told that Julie and Tom were going to get married, she said to Julie, "You're taking him away from me!" Rose was then in her early 70s. Julie remembers Rose saying such things as, "I'm in my virgin lair," when she was at her desk in the shop.

Many notes and business cards from society figures survive from those years. Benjamin Sonnenberg, the public relations magnate whose grand house in Gramercy Park contained the Sargent portrait of Millicent, Duchess of Sutherland—Rose's idol—wrote to Rose, "Thank you for the exciting experience seeing your house!" There is a business card with the name Hippolyte de Komaroff, Ancien Colonel de la Garde Imperiale; this may be one of the friends from "pre-Communist Russia" that Rose's nephew, Anthony Cumming, remembers her having.

A handwritten letter with the engraved heading, "Royal Jugoslav Legation, Washington," says, "My dear Miss Cummings [sic], It is a great pleasure for me to thank you warmly for your kind invitation in your lovely home during my visit to New York." And a note that is written in a bold, nearly indecipherable hand says "How very very sweet of you to have sent me those two extremely pretty landscapes." It is signed Princess Yvonne de Rothschild.

OPPOSITE
Ted Peckham, who is identified here as the owner of "an L.A. outfit called Super Gigolo Service," gave paid tea dances at the Waldorf-Astoria. Rose in middle age, still chaperoned by her mother, was frequently his partner.
Herald-Examiner Collection, Los Angeles Public Library.

Rose Cumming "Ivy," original hand-block print.
Photograph by Jayson K. T. Schwaller, Dessin Fournir Collections.

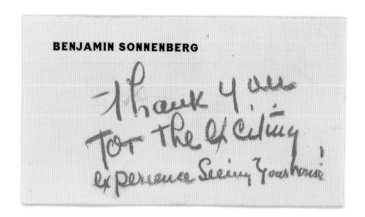

ABOVE Benjamin Sonnenberg was a press agent and impresario who made himself famous with clients such as CBS and the film producer David O. Selznick. John Singer Sargent's portrait of Rose's idol, the Duchess of Sutherland, hung in Sonnenberg's Grammercy Park mansion. *Courtesy of Sarah Cumming Cecil.*

There was a degree of desperation in all this activity, however. It is not clear, for instance, whether Rose hoped the Princess de Rothschild would buy the landscapes she sent or whether they were a gesture of thanks for favors already done.

A man named Langdon Marvin, who lived at 40 East Seventy-sixth Street, wrote to Rose the day after Christmas in 1937:

Dear Rose,

You send me such delightful Christmas gifts with such charming appreciation of what you call my 'kindnesses,' but I have a feeling that I may have left much undone that should have been done for you. I do hope matters are going better & shall count on you to let me know if I can help. The little figures are exquisite, with their ages old charm, and they stand on our mantel to delight the eye and soul.

Many thanks, indeed, and all good wishes.

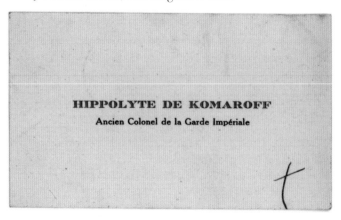

ABOVE Rose had many friends among the dispossessed Russian aristocracy. *Courtesy of Sarah Cumming Cecil.*

Rose was never loathe to promote herself or her business, but an advertisement from the late 1930s in which she endorsed a line of tables made by the Imperial Furniture Company in Grand Rapids, Michigan, seems something of a comedown from the usual newspaper mention of her buying or selling antiques and paintings. The headline reads: "If I had less than $50 to spend for Furniture," says Rose Cumming, "I would buy a table." This is next to a photograph of Rose looking distinctly louche, wearing a broad-brimmed hat, leaning up against a fireplace with one arm akimbo on a thrust out hip. One hopes she was paid a lot, even in Depression dollars, to lend her name to the tables.

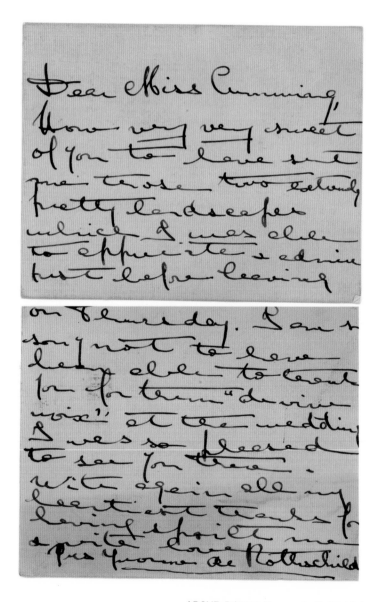

ABOVE Princess Yvonne de Rothschild thanks Rose for two landscapes. It is not clear if Rose sold them to her or gave them to her, perhaps as an investment in future decorating work. *Courtesy of Sarah Cumming Cecil.*

There are two letters from 1939 that indicate that just as the enormous personal change of leaving Australia coincided with the beginning of World War I in the lives of the Cumming girls, so there was another tremendous personal change in their lives just as World War II was about to start: they lost their mother. Sarah Fennell Hughes Cumming had begun life on a sheep ranch and ended it after 20 years of living in Manhattan. She had been an affectionate mother, a warm and gracious hostess, and an anchor in Rose's life. The change went deep, marking the indelible placement of Rose in middle age and leaving her alone in a way she had never been. Eileen and Dorothy had husbands and children; Rose from now on had only admirers.

One of the sympathy letters to Rose on the death of her mother is from a friend named Ruth. It is full of empathy and support. Ruth had apparently sent flowers because Rose, characteristically practical, wrote across the corner of the letter "Red Roses," presumably as an aide memoire for a thank-you note.

The other letter is representative of Rose's mixture of the professional and the personal. The head of the letter is "GRACIE Antiques-Old Prints-Screens-Lamps-Art Goods," and it is signed "Mr. Gracie." Gracie antique wallpapers is a firm that survives today. The 1939 letter from Mr. Gracie reads:

Dear Miss Cummings [sic],

It was very distressing to me to read of the loss of your mother. Many times I have remarked to friends of your affection to your mother and it will live with me for a long time. You must feel happy in the thought you had her with you for so many years. I lost my mother when I was seven and never did know what a mother was. Let us hope we will see them later on.

With the advent of World War II in Europe and the Blitz over England, Dorothy, her husband, Allan McNab, and her sons,

Tony and Greville, came back to the United States. Tony was devoted to Rose. He explains why:

One memory which really lingers is that at the age of six [in approximately 1930] we were living in Southampton and I came down with a mastoid problem which today would require nothing more than a shot of penicillin[,] but at that time was quite difficult and necessitated a serious operation. Rose came to the New York hospital and seeing my distress[,] fear[,] and even terror of these (to me) medical ghouls and associated operating equipment comforted me[,] at which time I latched on to her with an enormous hug saying "save me" etc. It apparently bonded her to me and she never forgot it. I believe her future generosity in all things to me was rooted from that moment.

Reminiscing about the early war years, Tony says:

When we left England we brought Mr. Cantor, a popeyed Pekinese[,] back with us [the dog was named for Eddie Cantor, the popular singer known for his bug-eyed look] and left him with Aunt Rose who loved him madly. I believe in many ways he ruined her life as she had always shopped the world for antiques and due to dog and rabies restrictions could not take him with her to various countries, so she stopped her trips until he died which was after the war. The shopping was out anyway due to the war so it was [perhaps] not a terrible loss.

Rose sat out the war behind her magical windows on Madison Avenue and Fifty-third Street. One day, in 1945, a young man from Tennessee walked into her shop. His name was Albert Hadley.

OPPOSITE Rose's genius for self promotion sometimes took her down strange roads. In the Depression every penny counted, so Rose, looking blasé and sophisticated, endorsed some homely Grand Rapids reproduction tables. *Dessin Fournir Collections.*

The formidable Gertrude Stein sits enthroned in her Paris salon in a chair with a Rose Cumming slipcover (see opposite page).
Photograph by Henri Manuel, courtesy of Staley-Wise Gallery. New York.

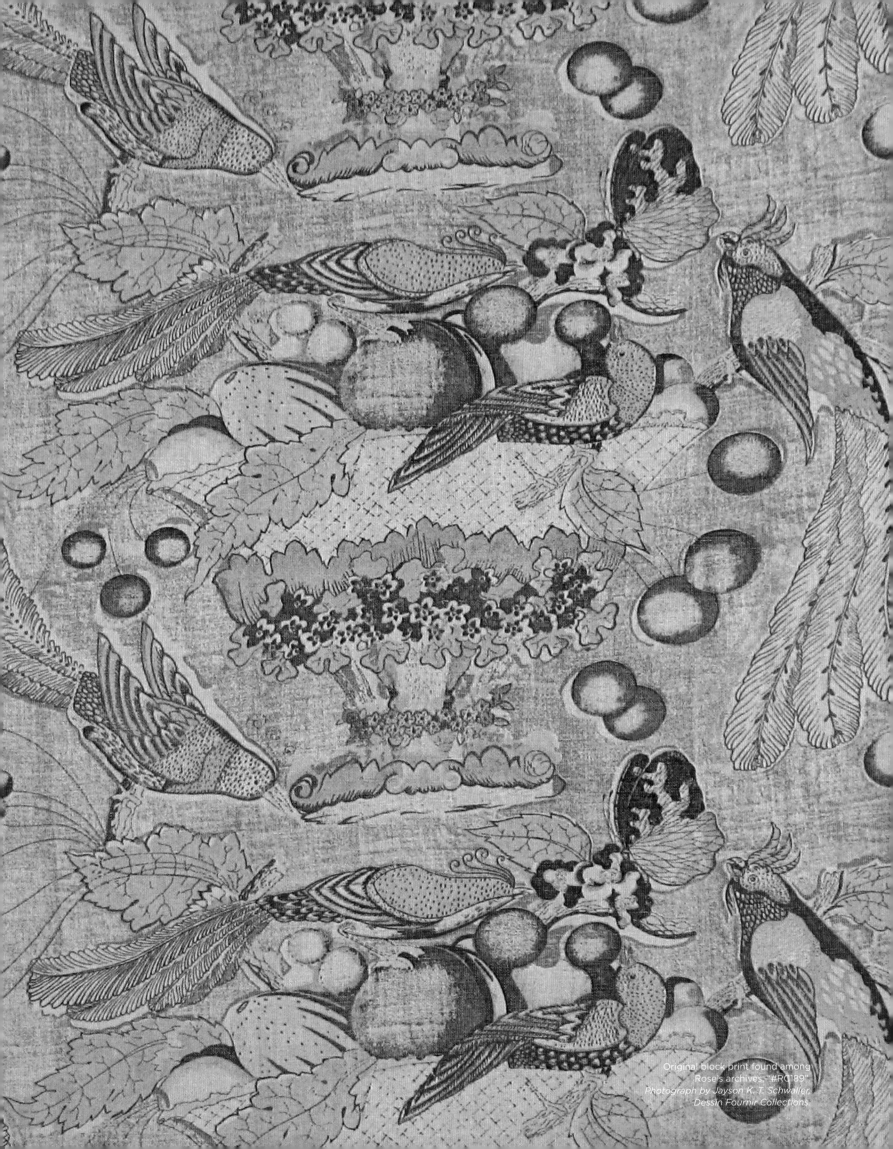

Black pred
of things in
White
$no o

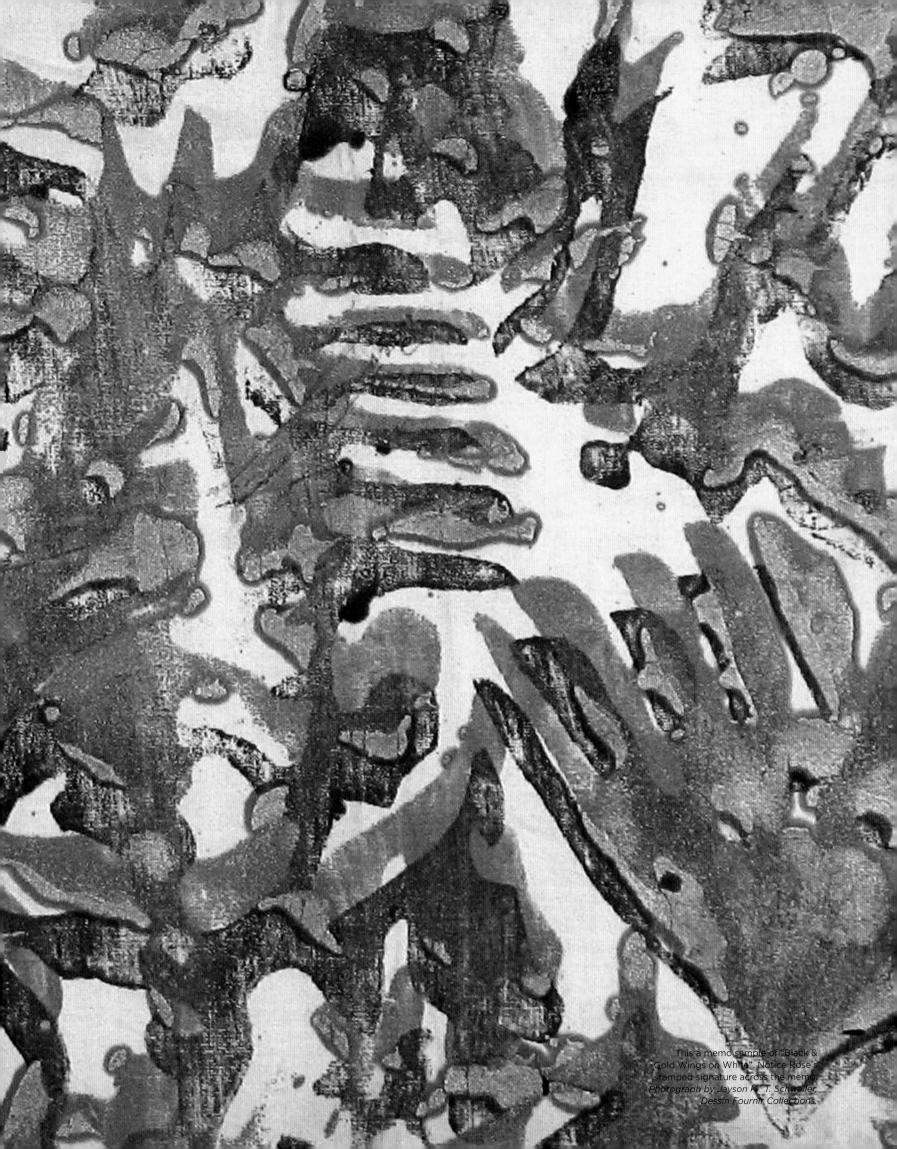

This a memo sample of "Black & Gold Wings on White". Notice Rose's stamped signature across the memo.
Photograph by Jayson K. T. Schwaller
Dessin Fournir Collections.

What was so astounding about her taste was that it was so off the wall. I mean it was reptiles, and there was a sort of Hollywood chic to it, but then there was sort of the macabre thing going on, and none of it was consistent, but they were things you had never seen before...

Bunny Williams, interior designer

OPPOSITE Designer James Amster created an enclave of town houses off New York's East Forty-ninth Street in 1944, where most of the pantheon of the design world gathered for a party. Left to right: Amster, Marian Hall, Ruby Ross Wood, Billy Baldwin (a fellow resident of "Amster Yard"), William Pahlmann, Dorothy Draper, Nancy McClelland. *Billy Baldwin Collection, courtesy of Adam Lewis.*

CHAPTER EIGHT

The Forties

Albert Hadley, who would go on to become one of the most respected interior designers in the world and one of the two iconic names of the famous firm Parish Hadley, remembers when he first met Rose Cumming:

Well, I met her the first summer I came to New York in 1945 I guess it was, and I was here on my way back to Nashville. I had been spending some time with friends in Maine. Basically[,] I had never been to New York before and there were so many people like Miss Rose that I wanted to meet—Billy Baldwin, Bill Pahlman, Ruby Ross Wood—you know, the whole gang. So Miss Rose's shop, as you know, the shop on Fifty-thrid and Madison: there was no D&D [Design and Decoration Building] in those days. The decorators were in the building across the street. So anyway, Miss Rose's shop was fantastic. I mean the chandeliers were hanging and marvelous furniture and over the door was that famous cat. I don't know if they still have that or not…well, that big porcelain cat. Madison Avenue is here. The front door was here. This is all glass and then there was glass all the way here and Miss Rose's desk was right there so as one walked by you could see this woman with her blue hair and all these things sparkling in the background. It was summer. No air conditioning but she had all these electric fans (I don't know how many of them), and they were all aimed at the chandeliers so there was a tinkling sound. Anyway, I went in and I think there were a couple of women there—they were tourists, and I was sort of standing in the background and a conversation started [between Miss Rose and me]: "Can you believe it? They bought an old candy-box. I just finished the chocolates today!" And I said, "What do you mean?" And she said, "Well, they loved the box, and they asked the price, and I told them."

So that was the beginning of our relationship, and we got along from the beginning. I mean it was just fantastic, and I also went on to meet all the other people I wanted to meet. I saw everybody because I let them know that I was not looking for a job, but that it was for admiration and that sort of thing. So I was very lucky. But Miss Rose was one of the top people on my list.

Rose's shop at Fifty-third and Madison was in the heart of the design district of the day. Across the street there was a building with designers' offices and "To the Trade" fabric companies. Leonard Stanley, a Los Angeles designer who knew Rose when he was young in New York, remembers that "Freddie Victoria," meaning Frederick P. Victoria, the antiques dealer and maker of reproductions whose firm still flourishes in the third generation, was across the street. A blurb written about the Victoria firm says that they were located there from 1941 to 1999. The same blurb, talking about Frederick Victoria's immediate return to France to shop for antiques after World War II, has a description that could very well apply to Rose: "it was a time when with a small amount of capital, a large amount of daring and, most importantly, a good eye a dealer could source astonishing things."

At some point in the late 1930s or early 1940s, Rose added cut flowers to her inventory. To keep them fresh—and because she missed no opportunity for drama—she installed constantly running sheets of water cascading down the windows on the Fifty-third Street side of the shop. The flowers had disappeared by the time anyone now living remembers the shop, although the pipes at the top of the windows and the trough at the bottom remained, but the "Niagara Falls" on the window are referred to in old letters. Rose told Thomas Britt that she had the flowers in the early days of World War II so that soldiers could "give a posy" to their girls.

Interior design was a well-established business by the time of World War II. The people that Albert Hadley says he wanted to meet when he came to town—Billy Baldwin, Bill Pahlman, Ruby Ross Wood—were pillars of the design establishment. Ruby Ross Wood, of course, had been the ghostwriter for Elsie de Wolfe in the second decade of the century and then an author and very successful decorator

in her own right. Billy Baldwin, who worked for Ruby Ross Wood from 1935 until her death in 1950, was known for his restrained Modernist style and his famous high-style clients such as Cole Porter, Pauline de Rothschild (who was also a customer in Rose's shop), the famous hostess Kitty Miller, the famous beauty Babe Paley, and Mrs. Paul Mellon. And Bill Pahlman was, from 1936 to 1942, head of the decorating and antiques department of Lord & Taylor. Mark Hampton says of this landmark position in design history:

[At Lord & Taylor, Pahlman] set out on a phase of his career that reached thousands of people through the immensely popular model rooms that he created for the store. Attendance was huge, and so was the publicity. From then on the development of Pahlman's style was followed closely by newspapers and magazines all over the country. This famous style, which became the epitome of fifties design, embodied the anticlassicism and freedom from the past that characterized the modern movements of the early part of the twentieth century. Its chief focus was on the mixture of unexpected visual elements, creating an effect that editors and writers invariably described as "dramatic," "spectacular," and "daring." Accompanying these…assemblages were color schemes of an equally daring and surprising nature: red, orange, sky blue and lime green, or dark brown, olive green, pale blue, and terra cotta. He loved surprises and what Robert Hughes calls the "shock of the new."

What is significant in design history about Albert Hadley's list is that two of the people on it were men. Interior design in America had been established by women—Elsie de Wolfe and Edith Wharton to begin with—and then developed as a profession by other strong women who had professional ethics and a solid clientele, usually of society women. Ruby Ross Wood and Eleanor Brown at McMillen are good examples. And, of course, there was Rose in a class by herself.

It was not until the time of World War II and afterward that men had an identity in the design world. And furthermore, it was not until William Pahlman got attention for his model rooms at Lord & Taylor that designers courted publicity as an end in itself. The model rooms were publicized almost as performances. They were not somebody's home that

OPPOSITE One of the many chandeliers Rose had hanging in the shop. Mark Hampton said that, although they tended to be rusty and "messily draped with crystal," they were "divine in their weird way." Rose kept fans trained on them, so that they would stir in the breeze. *Dessin Fournir Collections.*

happened to be photographed and published. They were created for the purpose of publicity.

Among women decorators, Dorothy Draper was the exception in terms of deliberately cultivating attention for her work and herself as a design personality, but her newspaper columns and books mostly appeared after World War II.

Rose alone straddled the divide between the genteel women designers with their whiff of disdain for public attention and later designers whose personalities were as big as their work—people in the last third of the twentieth century such as Mario Buatta, "the Prince of Chintz," and the curmudgeonly Sister Parish who decorated the Kennedy White House. Rose had a solid design practice, particularly in the 1920s and 1930s, but she was always larger than life, an extravagant personality—"self-created like Coco Chanel," "her talent the equivalent of Garbo's face"—so that she came to embody creativity in her own person. Her shop and her house were their own kind of model rooms.

Albert Hadley says "as a personality and a woman of great style and great aesthetic qualities, great taste if you will…I mean she was superb. There was nobody like her."

The lady designers hated her for her style, and she had no time for them. Albert Hadley says, "I got to McMillen and was working with Eleanor Brown and all those lady decorators and none of them could believe that this Rose would be nice to me. None of them could go in there because she shunned them so. She wanted to get them out. She didn't want those lady decorators in her shop."

Rose's allegiance to her family, particularly to her two sisters, was one of the strongest and most persistent threads through her life. Russell Cecil, Eileen's son, says that when he was a boy, he and his mother "used to go [to Rose's shop] practically every day because my mother and Rose tried to see each other very regularly. Daily was fine but three times a week would be a minimum."

Eileen, the most conventional of the sisters—a typical middle child one could say—had, as we have noted, a successful and glamorous career of her own. She worked at *Vogue* and *Harper's Bazaar*, and, in 1925 when Mr. Gimbel was opening Saks Fifth Avenue, he asked her to be publicity and design director. Eileen's warmth seems to

OPPOSITE
Town & Country, the arbiter of taste for old money, shows a model reflected in the windows of Rose's Madison Avenue shop. *Photograph by Gleb Derujinsky,* Town & Country, *February 1955.*

be as much remembered as Rose's high style and occasional *froideur*. Albert Hadley says that after Rose died in 1968, "Mrs. Cecil was there...sort of taking over and she would wear some of Miss Rose's big hats and then she tried to look like Miss Rose, but she never did. Never did quite make it. She was charming though. I liked her."

Degrees of charm and style notwithstanding, all three sisters were extraordinary women. Their accomplishments—actress, design director, internationally known decorator—would have been remarkable coming from any background. Coming from the ends of the earth to America where they knew no one, they were a unique triumvirate. Dorothy's son, Anthony Cumming, says "the more I think about Aunt Rose, Aunt Eileen and my mother, the more I realize how extraordinary they were."

Rose and Eileen, in addition to their family allegiance, maintained a strong feeling for Australia, and, when they could, they used their contacts in the New York society world to benefit their native land—and to enhance their own visibility. In 1942, there was a fund-raising dinner given at the Waldorf-Astoria on April 24, the day before the national Australian holiday in honor of ANZAC, the Australian and New Zealand Army Corps that performed so valiantly in World War I. The *New York Times* for April 12, 1942, noted:

Miss Rose Cumming...is in charge of arrangements for the dinner, which commemorates the landing, in 1915, of Australian and New Zealand forces at Gallipoli. A feature of the evening will be the showing of motion pictures of the countries before and after the declaration of the current war. Others on the arrangements committee are Mrs. Russell Cecil, etc., etc....

Proceeds from the dinner will be divided between the British War Relief Society Australian Comforts Fund and its New Zealand National Patriotic Fund aiding the united forces in the South Pacific combat zone. Lord Halifax, the British Ambassador, will be guest of honor and principal speaker.

Correspondence survives between Rose and a Mr. McCormick-Goodhart, honorary attaché to the British Embassy in Washington about the order of seating at the dinner. Mr. McCormick-Goodhart wrote to Rose on April 20, four days before the banquet: "You sent me quite a difficult task in your night letter of April 19th. However, I have taken the bull by the horns and enclose a list representing the order of your distinguished guests on Friday as well as I can from the left end facing your guest table to the right end." Across the top of this missive, Rose has written in red pencil, "Lord Halifax to be on my right."

As an indication of the mingling of the entertainment world and society, which took place then as now, Ruth Draper, the famous monologuist—and incidentally the sister-in-law of Dorothy Draper—was on Rose's committee for the banquet; and Gracie Fields, the beloved Old English music hall singer and comedienne who had performed for the troops in Australia, was flown in from California to perform. The tickets were ten dollars apiece.

Several months after the gala, a clipping was sent to Rose that had been published in *The Australian Comforts Fund Bulletin* and "throughout Australia in a great many newspapers." The account begins with a flourish of trumpets:

Particulars have just been received in Melbourne of what was described in New York as "the most brilliant event of its kind ever held in this city." This was the Anzac Dinner, which took place in the Waldorf-Astoria Hotel on the night of April 24, Anzac Eve. Nearly 1300 guests attended. Included among the many notabilities

Anzac Dinner

WALDORF-ASTORIA

FRIDAY, APRIL 24th AT SEVEN P.M.

I enclose my check for $............ for .... tickets
at $10.00 each.

Name..

Address..

PLEASE RESERVE TABLE FOR ☐ 12, ☐ 10, ☐ 8
Please make checks payable to
Anzac Division, The British War Relief Society, 730 Fifth Avenue, New York City
TABLE RESERVATIONS WILL BE GIVEN OUT AT DOOR

ABOVE ANZAC Day, April 25, is a national holiday in Australia and New Zealand held to commemorate the landing at Gallipoli on that date in 1915 of the Australian and New Zealand Army Corps. Rose and Eileen gave an ANZAC eve dinner in 1942 for the benefit of the British War Relief Society. *Courtesy of Sarah Cumming Cecil.*

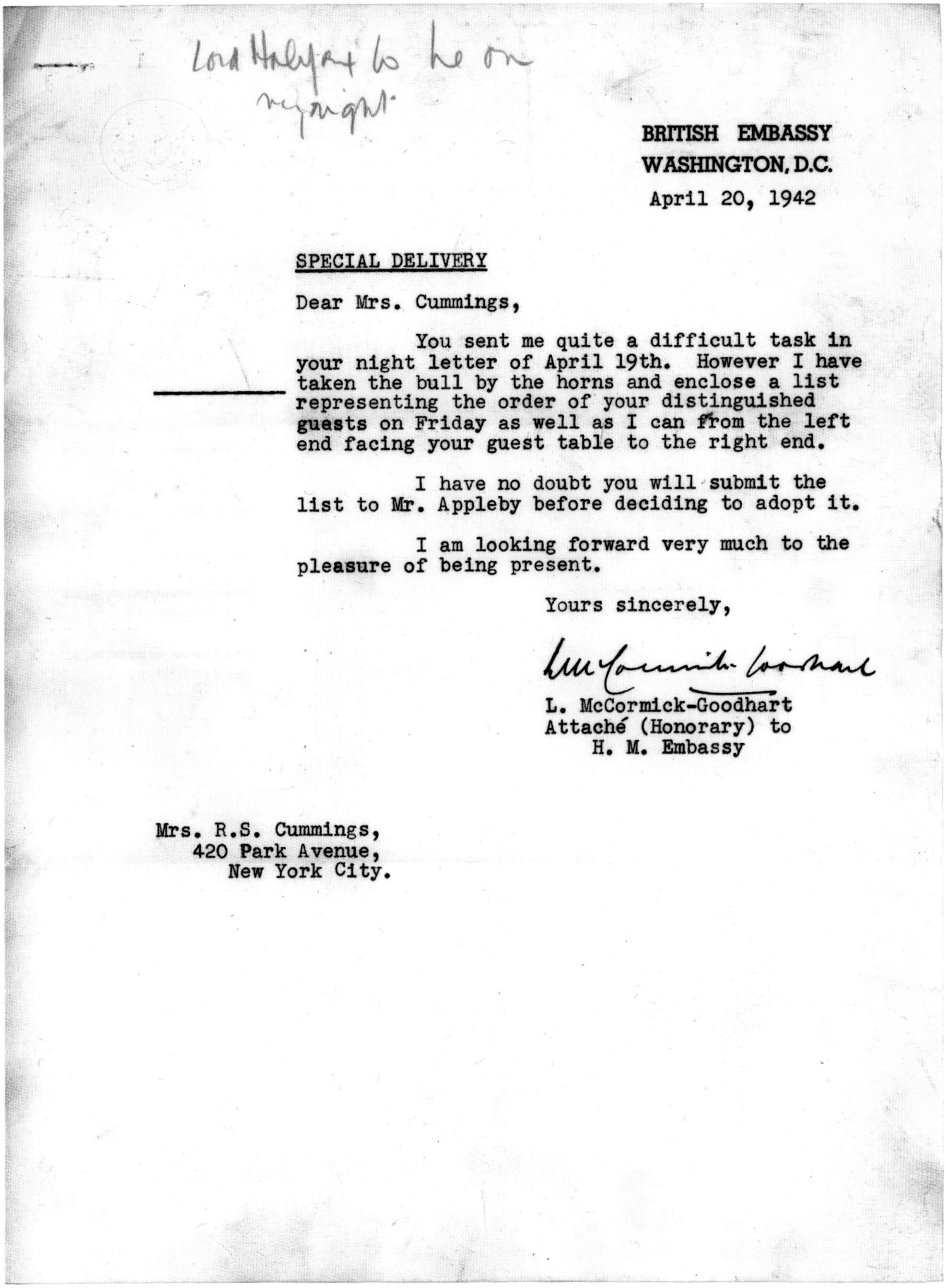

Lord Halifax to be on my right.

BRITISH EMBASSY
WASHINGTON, D.C.
April 20, 1942

SPECIAL DELIVERY

Dear Mrs. Cummings,

You sent me quite a difficult task in your night letter of April 19th. However I have taken the bull by the horns and enclose a list representing the order of your distinguished guests on Friday as well as I can from the left end facing your guest table to the right end.

I have no doubt you will submit the list to Mr. Appleby before deciding to adopt it.

I am looking forward very much to the pleasure of being present.

Yours sincerely,

L. McCormick-Goodhart
Attaché (Honorary) to
H. M. Embassy

Mrs. R.S. Cummings,
420 Park Avenue,
New York City.

ABOVE An attaché to the British Embassy sent Rose a letter regarding the precedence for seating at the ANZAC dinner Rose and Eileen were giving. Characteristically, Rose wrote in red pencil "Lord Halifax [the British ambassador to Washington] to be on my right."
Courtesy of Sarah Cumming Cecil.

Australian Comforts Fund News of August 1942

In Honour of Australia

Brilliant New York Function

$20,000 Raised for A.C.F.

Particulars have just been received in Melbourne of what was described in New York as "the most brilliant event of its kind ever held in this city." This was the Anzac Dinner, which took place in the Waldorf-Astoria Hotel on the night of April 24, Anzac Eve. Nearly 1300 guests attended. Included among the many notabilities present were Viscount Halifax, Field-Marshal Sir John Dill, Mr. Wendell Wilkie, Baron de Rothschild, the Hon. H. V. Evatt, and the Ministers in the United States for New Zealand, South Africa and Canada.

Great enthusiasm prevailed. Addresses were given by Sir John Dill, Lt.-General Henry H. Arnold, Dr. Evatt and Mr. Walter Nash. Gracie Fields flew from California to give special entertainment for the guests, and moving pictures of Australia and New Zealand were shown.

Not the least important result of the dinner was the raising of $20,000 for the Australian Comforts Fund, and $5,000 for the New Zealand Patriotic Fund. The function was sponsored by the British War Relief Society of New York, but much of the credit for organising the dinner must go to two Australian women now resident in America. They are Miss Rose Cumming, one of New York's leading interior decorators, and her sister, Mrs. Russell Cecil, wife of a well-known doctor. They were Chairman and Co-Chairman respectively of the Dinner Committee, which was composed of men and women prominent in New York social and business life.

Mr. John Curtin, Prime Minister of Australia, is patron of the Anzac Division of the British War Relief Society. Until recently, this Division was a separate organisation, known as the Anzac War Relief Fund, and for many months it has been doing excellent work in America on behalf of Australian and New Zealand fighting forces.

ABOVE An Australian newspaper article celebrating the success of Rose and Eileen's ANZAC dinner, which raised $25,000 1942 dollars. Rose is described as "one of New York's leading interior decorators." Australian Conforts Fund News, *August 1942, courtesy of Sarah Cumming Cecil.*

present were Viscount Halifax, Field-Marshall Sir John Dill, Mr. Wendell Wilkie, Baron de Rothschild, the Hon. H.V. Evatt, and the Ministers in the United States for New Zealand, South Africa and Canada…

Not the least important result of the dinner was the raising of $20,000 for the Australian Comforts Fund, and $5000 for the New Zealand Patriotic Fund…much of the credit for organizing the dinner must go to two Australian women now resident in America. They are Miss Rose Cumming, one of New York's leading interior decorators, and her sister, Mrs. Russell Cecil, wife of a well-known doctor. They were Chairman and Co-Chairman respectively of the Dinner Committee, which was composed of men and women prominent in New York social and business life.

Rose's nephews, Dorothy's sons, Anthony and Greville, were in the military, as was Jack Hughes, the son of the sisters' half brother, Frederick Hughes who lived in Australia. Greville Cumming was killed in the war. Two letters survive from Jack Hughes, one to Eileen and Dr. Cecil and one to Rose. They are both from 1944. Jack was in love with a young woman named Janet in New York, and he tried repeatedly to bring her and Rose together as friends.

Jack's first letter:

Dearest Eilly & Russ:

Sorry to have been so long in answering your letter, which came last week. Thanks so much for sending the flowers dear. She [Janet] was thrilled to death with them.

I wished to have read Rose's letter after spending the evening with Janet. Sheer dismay on her part. But then as Janet said, I am like "the little girl with the curl."

ABOVE Dorothy Cumming McNab, the former silent screen star, with her son, Greville, who was killed in World War II.
Courtesy of Sarah Cumming Cecil.

The implication here is that Rose and Janet's evening was not a success, and Janet is assuming the blame for it since it was said of "the little girl with the curl…when she was good, she was very, very good, and when she was bad, she was horrid." The debacle may not have been all Janet's fault, however, because in later years Rose was known to be charming to young men and often the reverse to young women. Jack's letter continues, "[Janet] brings out the best in me. No I did not say beast. Be nice to her Eilly. She means an awful lot in my life, and I like her influence."

Later in the letter, Jack says, "Do you think we could stretch the [ration] points for a little dinner the night I get home[?] About twelve including yourselves. Janet, Baby, Jean Sterling and a few others. Would like to have Lele Daly—she is such fun at a party and will probably stop Rose's tears."

Jack's other surviving letter, directed to Rose, has the classic soldier's heading, done for security reasons, "Somewhere in France." Jack apparently tried to have Janet live in Rose's house, and, not too surprisingly to everyone but Jack, it did not work.

Dearest Rose,

Your cable arrived late last night and a V mail about three days ago. This was the one which told me Janet had moved from the house to take a place of her own. Was sorry to hear the news—as I thought it would be grand companionship for you both. Especially you, as I believe you spend too much time alone. Janet is so gay and vivacious and is good for you…

Life is a continual series of forward moves & racing to keep them in range. They retreat away from our fire and then we catch them again for some more blasting. One of these days it must all suddenly end and collapse. I doubt if the people themselves will fight. There will be some sniping and Nazi guerillas but that will quickly stop. My choice is for the ruthless Russians to get there first, and that has been their fear all along. It would do them a world of good to have those killers there before us.

From what we hear here, New York seems to be very gay and attractive…You always speak of wanting me to stay with you. When I come home, I will do that for a short period. Until I get settled, buy some clothes, and save a few dollars. Then I want to have one of the most attractive apts., I can get, make it my home, and settle down to enjoying it. I've done so long now without anything attractive & nice in my life—I have spent many an hour going over this apt. piece by piece. When I get thru, aided and abetted by the Rose Cumming touch, it ought to be a "lulu"…

You never mention any business details, so I never know if you are doing well or on the verge. But I always hope it is the former. Things ought to be easier for you now though.

Not much more news, Rose dear. Keep your chin up and I'll keep my head down.

[M]y fondest love. I think of you all, all the time

[Y]our devoted

Jack

Rose was very attached to all her nephews—Jack Hughes, Russell Cecil, Greville Cumming and, of course, Anthony Cumming. Anthony has a memory of the kind of extravagant gesture Rose was prone to.

One time when I went to Rose's shop she said, "I have something for you" and then produced a very large overcoat [Anthony Cumming is 6 feet 4 inches tall]. It was black with a fur collar and the entire lining was sable (as was the collar). Apparently one of her impoverished Russian friends had fallen on hard times and asked her if she would buy it as he desperately needed the money. She gave him what he needed (and probably more) and then gave the coat to me. I wore it once to a party in Tuxedo on a bitter cold night but never again. About two weeks later she asked if she could have it back and said the friend had come in to see her and was freezing, so of course she gave it back to him—free—and that was the end of that, classic Rose helping as usual. She had a remarkably soft heart and was frequently taken advantage of by a sob story.

As to Jack's question about how Rose's business is going, the answer was probably not too well. There would have been no decorating during the war, and it seems that Rose let that part of her business mostly lapse after the war. She concentrated on the fabrics and the antiques.

A letter from a London antiques dealer and longtime supplier of fabrics, dated February 7, 1946, indicates that Rose was very much involved in importing as soon as peacetime permitted her. It also mentions, as Tony Cumming frequently does, Rose's kindness.

The printed head of the letter is "3 Chelsea Embankment, London, S.W.3," over which "Alfie," the correspondent, has written "River House."

My dear Rose—

I cannot thank you enough & feel very touched by the kind thought of sending me that delightful parcel of lovely delicious things—very much appreciated—the first & only one I have ever had—I do think it was very sweet of you…[I] have managed to get some really lovely good second hand curtains of the best…it is the only way to get good material here as everything is for export and the [stuff?] left to us is rotten and not worth the expense of making up—my collection of French and Italian brocades is really great—some really good silk damask curtains quite like old days—I have a Turk & Italian who go to all the sales & give me the first pick before they go anywhere—as I dealt with them before the war…

[I had] windows with shutters so I had no blackout to do during the bombing—& I [was] lucky enough to lose only three small panes of glass—in spite of being in the main road of the bombers & doodle bugs [these were particularly vicious self-propelled bombs that were introduced by the Germans in the Blitz of 1944]—the worst part of all was the black streets at night groping about with a torch—it was heaven when the lights went on—also sirens groaning got on one's nerves—however one has forgotten it all—the trouble now is this wretched Socialist gov't who are making a proper mess of everything & doing all they can to break up any luxury business—& they only got in by lying like troopers telling everyone that when they got in everything would be all right—no more [illegible]—houses for all—food in plenty—all of which is far worse now than it was during the war—& they are all beginning to be sorry they voted for them…

All the best Rose—& again a thousand thanks…always

[Y]ours ever

Alfie

P.S. The silk stockings were pinched out of the parcel—otherwise everything in order! It is awful the pilfering that goes on—I really cannot thank you enough for your kind thoughts—

Alfie

Painter Jeremiah Goodman, who knew Rose when he was a young man, has a story about Rose's business during the war—and by implication about her cash-flow problems. "They say [during the war that] she got US customs to impound her fabrics, and she couldn't have been happier about it because she didn't have to worry about storage, and she got them out piecemeal by piecemeal."

Jeremiah Goodman made Rose's acquaintance in a way that she later mythologized. In *A Door Always Open*, she wrote:

Having been forced to move my shop…from Madison Avenue to my present location on Park Avenue, I received many nice letters telling me of how people felt and wishing me success. One day, shortly after the move, as I was arranging things in the shop window, a young man went by, stopped, and retracing his steps walked through the open door. "Oh, Miss Cumming," he said, shaking my hand, "I'm so glad. It's wonderful to find you here. I didn't know where you were. Everyone has been asking."

A few days later I received a letter from him. He wrote, "Dear Miss Cumming; I'm writing you this letter and am not putting my address at the top because I have no axe to grind whatever, but I felt that I really had to write you and tell you what you have meant in my life. When I came to New York as a boy of 19, I was very poor, and I always loved to look at your windows. But more than that, I was so often hungry and seldom could have anything to eat at night, and whenever this happened I would think to myself: "What will I do?" So I'd go and look in your windows and come away refreshed. These are my memories."

I was surprised and greatly touched. I have never seen him since, and I wish I knew his name.

As you can see—there are all kinds of things that happen if you have a door always open.

Jeremiah, who says, "I was that young man," remembers things somewhat differently, although he fully agrees that Rose's windows were sustenance for him. He had come to New York in 1939 to go to art school, and he says,

I would just look at [Rose's] window. I was extremely unhappy. Very poor. I was living on about 60 cents a day. You could then… well, you had 5 cents for the subway, 15 cents for the breakfast which was fake orange juice, cinnamon doughnut and black coffee, and lunch was 25 or 30 cents and 5 cents for each vegetable…

I was living with an aunt and uncle in Brooklyn for two reasons— both honest. It was all my family could do to send me to art school in New York even though I had some scholarships…[T]he aunt was my father's sister, she was a sweet thing, she loved me but her husband certainly didn't because he was shelling out money for someone who [he] wasn't cozy about—me and my family. So I did live with them for a year…but it seemed like ten years…I went to school on Madison Avenue—400 Madison—which was called [the] Franklin School of Professional Art…I hated going back to Brooklyn. But in order to get back to Brooklyn I had to take the subway at Fifty-third and Madison and the entrance is still there. Rose's shop was on the corner. I used to go by her shop and I would do anything other than go back to Brooklyn to this hideous uncle of mine. I used to look at the windows of Rose's shop and after [a while] I really got to know every single thing in the windows, I knew the whole thing by memory.

I used to go to art school then go to the Museum of Modern Art for the movies and then that would be about 5:30 or 6:00 and I would take the subway. So I passed her windows all the time. She never knew me but she had obviously seen me looking in the windows… At one point she used to wave to me…

Jeremiah says that, rather than sending Rose an anonymous fan letter many years later, he told her what an important part her windows had played in his young life a few years later when he met her at a party. The party was given by Gordon Bolitho and his brother, Hector, who was a famous ballet critic from England. Gordon Bolitho was also a friend of Tilly Losch,

who played the concubine wife [in the movie The Good Earth*]. She was a dancer. If you see the movie, she was in it. She was also into other things. She was photographed by Cecil Beaton as well. I forget what the [party] was about…Rose Cumming wanted to meet Tilly Losch and whatever. I don't think anyone wanted to meet me.*

Jeremiah and Rose did become friends, however, as happened with many talented young men whom she met and fascinated. He said, "I used to go to her place for dinner, and she would just serve tomato soup because she said she liked the color of it in black bowls. She would bring out some saltine crackers."

Jeremiah admired Rose's spirit.

[She] had a law suit with the Crown Prince of Norway. She lived across from the Museum of Modern Art and during wartime she rented the top floors [of her house]…. She was really in a sense a slumlord. People complained bitterly about lack of heat or something, but she was a typical lady decorator. She couldn't have cared less that [it] was [the] Crown Prince of Norway and his wife, and they sued her and she would have none of it. And I think he lost. It was one of those "what you see is what you get." Anyone else would have been "Oh my god…they're royalty," and she couldn't have cared less.

Jeremiah has not remembered the titles or the date accurately, but he certainly got Rose's sang froid about the presence of royalty in her house. Her tenant was actually Prince Carl Johan Bernadotte, a grandson of the king of Sweden, who had arrived in New York by plane on February 5, 1946, according to the *New York Times*. He had come to marry Mrs. Kerstin Wijkmark, a Swedish woman and sometime journalist who, at 35, was six years older than the prince and who had been divorced twice. The whole affair was an eerie replay on a somewhat smaller scale of the Prince of Wales and Mrs. Simpson—eventually to become the Duke and Duchess of Windsor—ten years earlier. The couple was married in late February, and the king disowned his grandson, stripping him of all his royal titles and pregrogatives.

On October 6, 1946, the *Times* noted "Bernadotte Leases a Duplex. Prince Carl Johan Bernadotte has rented a duplex apartment in 36 West Fifty-third Street, from Rose Cumming, through Mary Lewis, broker."

Things went downhill from there. Sometime within two years the Prince and his wife, now Mr. and Mrs. Bernadotte, moved out and sued Rose for failure to provide services. He leased an apartment at 29 East Sixty-fourth Street on October 20, 1948; his wife made an unsuccessful suicide attempt there on December 23. The prince seems not to have chosen his women very wisely. Rose won the lawsuit.

What most impressed Jeremiah about Rose was her color sense—as was the case with many other design-world people who knew her—but Jeremiah, perhaps because he is a painter, has something to say about it that no one else has said.

She always did something that I thought was wonderful. She would take something like this piece here and love to put jewel colors against earth colors. And when you think about it, jewels come out of the earth and they sparkle. There's nothing more incredible … like I have some amethyst type glass…Murphy glass and other pieces but if you put those colors next to dirt colors… she was famous for using a lot of Chinese ceramics and things that were very muddy in color. Sometimes metallic colors but she would unhesitatingly think "Oh what a wonderful green this is!"

I'm fabricating but I have a feeling that she was the sort of person who didn't have to see a label … I think that's what her talent was … We're talking about emotional feeling.

Rose had that talent of being able to go from Fifty-thrid Street, go to Madison Avenue, but sometimes go up and down 3rd Avenue, which was a mess at that time with junk shops … None of them could exist today for one minute. And she forever would see something in a window — it could be a paper fan beat up whatever but if the color was right she sensed it. She inspired me incredibly by color.

I loved going to her town house, which was right across the street from the Museum of Modern Art. It was so fascinating and so beautiful. We would sit in that library with the dark green walls and all the marvelous colors and she always sat on the sofa and I would be facing her this way and chat or have a drink or whatever. Then the two of us would go down to the kitchen into the pantry and she would put it together and all her best china would come out—that's all she had. She didn't have anything but just beautiful things and we would sit at the mirrored top table in the dining room (this was on the ground floor) by the window on the street and the table was there and we would sit there and laugh[. S]he had a wicked sense of humor and was so entertaining[. S]he helped me a lot. She was always very supportive. She would give me advice in a stern way—what I should do and what I shouldn't.

[W]e would be talking about clients or something and [she would say] things like "You're the boss. You tell them what you want. It's all salesmanship." I mean that was her thing. She loved selling.

Albert Hadley, interior designer

OPPOSITE Rose, photographed with a come-hither look and her nimbus of hair, which by this time she was dying blue. *Photograph by T. J. Fitzsimmons.*

CHAPTER NINE

An Inspiration

By 1950, Rose's finances had fallen to a low ebb. With her customary genius for promoting herself, however, she turned what would have been a desperation measure for anyone else into a grand innovative gesture. Rose's nephew, Anthony Cumming, remembers through the haze of fond memories that her house "was a museum — it was so wonderful that people paid to see it." The real reason for his remark was trumpeted in the *Sunday Mirror Magazine*, affiliated with the English newspaper the *Daily Mirror*, of February 25, 1951: "Now the Tax Bogey Forces Open STATELY HOMES of MANHATTAN to Anybody With a Buck." Jerome Zerbe, a friend of Rose's as well as a photographer and decorative-arts writer, known for such books as *Les Pavillons: French Pavilions of the Eighteenth Century* and *The Art of Social Climbing*, wrote the article.

The wealthy folks of England — those who are left — a few years ago hit on a novel plan to save their ancient estates from the reaching fingers of high costs and high taxes that threatened to take them away. They simply opened their homes as public museums, charging a moderate fee to those who wished to see how the upper classes lived … Accordingly, at least one New Yorker has decided to take up the British plan and many others may follow her example.

The pioneer is Rose Cumming, one of the nation's leading interior decorators, who lives in a magnificent brownstone house on W. Fifty-third St. Every Sunday afternoon, from 4 o'clock until 8, anyone with $1 may drop in and browse around the fabulous mansion, admiring the splendid furnishings that make Miss Cumming's home one of the showplaces of the city.

OPPOSITE
Rose, with her genius for self-promotion, managed to turn her desperate financial straits, which had led to her opening her home to tours for a dollar, into a feature article in the English *Sunday Mirror Magazine*, a supplement of the very popular *Daily Mirror.* Sunday Mirror Magazine, *February 25, 1951 courtesy of Mirrorpix.*

Manhattan Island lays claim to many of the world's great homes.

Now the Tax Bogey Forces Open
Stately Homes of Manhattan
to Anybody With a Buck

Rose Cumming, owner of the beautiful home, arrived in New York in 1917 from Australia to become one of the nation's top decorators.

...ville of the Sixteenth...

wealthy folks of England—those who are left—a few years ago hit on a novel plan to save their ancient estates from the reaching fingers of high costs and high taxes that threatened to take them away.

They simply opened their homes as public museums, charging a moderate fee to those who wished to see how the upper classes lived. The scheme met with considerable success, making Lord Vere de Vere very happy that he could retain the family holdings, and giving an inexpensive treat to the middle and lower income groups.

While as yet taxes in this country have not approached the almost confiscatory figures of Britain, it seems certain they will go higher before they drop. Accordingly, at least one New Yorker has decided to take up the British plan and many others may follow her example.

The pioneer is Rose Cumming, one of the nation's leading interior decorators, who lives in a magnificent brownstone house on W. 53d St. Every Sunday afternoon, from 4 o'clock until 8, anyone with $1 may drop in and browse around the fabulous mansion, admiring the splendid furnishings that make Miss Cumming's home one of the showplaces of the city.

Of recent years Miss Cumming has been besieged by museum directors and curators to open the home for public inspection and these pleas, too, have played a part in her decision.

Visitors to the Cumming home step into an entrance hall where a

walls are hung with two gorgeous old Italian paintings from the Eighteenth Century. The dining room is Early Georgian, with Regency furniture and decorations. It is completely mirrored in Venetian Roccaille.

The second floor hall is adorned with Oriental and English ornaments of the Eighteenth Century, including a Chinese bronze pagoda from Kang Hsi temple and a bronze Indo-Chinese urn holding the tree of life. The music room contains Eighteenth Century Oriental, Continental and English furniture, paintings and rare Bibelots. The drawing room is in rare French furniture and Oriental art, while the library is finished in English furniture, portraits and objects of art from the Eighteenth and early Nineteenth Centuries.

Miss Cumming is the daughter of a wealthy rancher from New South Wales, Australia. She came to New York in 1917 to visit a sister, now Mrs. Allan McNab, wife of the writer. The sister was then acting with a company on tour, so Rose took a job in the Census Bureau while waiting. By the time her sister returned to New York, Rose had become so fascinated with New York life that she was already knee deep in interior decoration and it was not long before she gave up the idea of returning to Australia.

Another sister, Aileen, is the wife of the well-known physician, Dr. Russell Cecil, who lives in a home almost as gorgeous as Rose's —which is no surprise, considering that Rose did the decorating.

PHOTOS BY HAROLD HALIDAY COSTAIN

Magnificent Louis XV crystal chandelier with leaf-shaped pendants and globular finial dominates the handsomely furnished library...

And then, with a bravura flourish: "Of recent years Miss Cumming has been besieged by museum directors and curators to open the home for public inspection and these pleas, too, have played a part in her decision."

The article continues with a mention of some of the outstanding pieces of art and furniture and concludes by saying:

Miss Cumming is the daughter of a wealthy rancher from New South Wales, Australia. She came to New York in 1917 to visit a sister, Mrs. Allan McNab, wife of the writer. The sister was then acting with a company on tour...By the time her sister returned to New York, Rose had become so fascinated with New York life that she was already knee deep in interior decoration and it was not long before she gave up the idea of returning to Australia. Another sister, Eileen, is the wife of the well-known physician, Dr. Russell Cecil, who lives in a home almost as gorgeous as Rose's—which is no surprise, considering that Rose did the decorating.

There is an aerial photograph of Manhattan captioned "Manhattan Island lays claim to many of the world's great homes"; a photograph of one of Rose's rooms with her signature gleaming parquet floor, Portuguese Queen Anne chair, and a crystal chandelier; and a large photograph of a plump Rose, smirking under an Adrian hat festooned with veiling.

A mimeographed set of pages survive that were given to people taking the tour. There is no way of knowing at this distance how many gawkers tramped through the rooms, but the front page of the homemade catalogue has the sad little statement framed in dots at the bottom: "Admission $1.00. Please use garden entrance."

Rose did nothing without the best provenance and pedigree she could contrive. Consequently, the essay on the first page of the catalogue is signed "Karl Freund." Freund was a German film cinematographer and director who shot such groundbreaking German Expressionist films as *The Golem* and *Metropolis*; in this country he shot *Dracula* and *Key Largo*, and he won an Academy Award for Best Cinematography for *The Good Earth*. Freund was also an old friend of Rose, with whom he shared a passion for the best antique furniture. An account in the *New York Times*, for February 21, 1924, lists an auction of the "Karl Freund Collection" and says that the first session brought $21,659.50, a staggering sum in those days. Rose is named as one of the buyers. Here we catch a glimpse of Rose's intersecting worlds with Jeremiah Goodman's memory of meeting Rose at the party given for Tilly Losch who played the concubine in *The Good Earth*, photographed by Karl Freund.

Freund's essay is a smoothly persuasive piece of advertising copy, which presents this public access to the house as a long sought and rare privilege. It is worth quoting in its entirety:

People from all over the country have frequently asked Rose Cumming, the renowned decorator, how she lived, what were her predilections, what sort of art objects did she care for and keep for herself for constant companions, and they have often asked her to let them go through her house and garden to find out the guiding inspiration of her life after business hours.

Until now it has only been feasible to invite friends and a few strangers whose houses she had furnished. More and more frequently Rose Cumming has been urged by Museum directors and curators, as well as by prominent educators, to open her house for inspection to the public and she has now yielded to these friendly suggestions.

The main purpose of this brochure is to serve as a brief catalogue of the highlights of what the visitor can expect to see and study for beauty of line and color, as well as historic appeal.

It is noteworthy that Freund introduces an educational aspect to Rose's work and that the beauty of line and color achieved is promoted as part of its appeal.

The objects in the following paragraphs are picked at random among the hundreds of fascinating and aristocratic objects of arts and crafts which are inhabitants of these beautiful rooms. We call them inhabitants because they animate the interiors by their sheer presence. They all are thoroughbreds conveying imagination, good taste and pure architectural proportions, which are the artistic heritage of bygone centuries.

It is almost as though Freund, here, sees the furniture and objects ("the inhabitants") as actors in one of his films who "animate the interiors" and whose spatial relations to each other are part of their dramatic presentation.

The House of Rose Cumming can boast with justification of its international atmosphere, of the fact that it brings centuries of artistry and artisanry together to create the perfect comfort of home, free of the orthodox "period" imprisonment.

We cannot give a complete inventory of the contents of the house in this limited space, but here are some of the chapters of romance and history which the great craftsmen of old prophetically composed for Rose Cumming to take their rightly place in the interiors of lofty rooms, parquet floors and wonderful old mantel pieces, eighteen in number, framing open fireplaces, the natural, almost paternal, focus of any room. To these objects of her choice she longs to come back after the arduous planning for the keenly appreciative American home lovers.

Thomas Britt remembers Rose's house at its peak, not long after she opened it to the public. He had walked into Rose's shop about ten years after Albert Hadley and after a brief exchange, Tom remembers Rose saying, "Come closer, come closer."

Tom said, "Good morning, Miss Cumming."

"The name is Rose!"

Rose then locked the shop and for the next hour proceeded to "bestow" on him "all these fabulous silks and hangings from the whole world of Chinese and Indian fabrics." She also issued an invitation to her by-then-legendary house, which had him "in seventh heaven." Tom says that he remembers Rose's house "as though it was yesterday." Looking at the illustrated article Rose wrote for the May 1928 *Arts & Decoration* magazine called "An Old Brownstone Building Transformed," he saw many changes between the house as Rose presented it in 1928 and what he saw almost 30 years later. Rose had said that the entrance hall was "narrow and irregular" and therefore difficult to make interesting. Her solution in 1928 was to put a large coromandel screen near the foot of the stairs, opposite "an old painting of a family group." By Tom's day, the entrance hall had completely changed. There was no coromandel screen, and he says, "the staircase in this article was all torn out. See, in the [1928] picture there is a machine-made nineteenth-century door and moldings. That was ripped out later when I knew her."

OPPOSITE The music room at the front of Rose's parlor floor with a Regency portrait and one of Rose's beautifully worn old rugs. *Dessin Fournir Collections.*

Rose's legendary drawing room papered in eighteenth-century Chinese silver paper that was decorated in tempera with trees, blossoms, birds, and figures. The Louis XV chaise longue was made by Pierre Bara, who entered the Paris guild of ebenistes in 1758. *Dessin Fournir Collections.*

He makes an interesting comment on the development of Rose's style. "It was all glamour when I knew her. So even Miss Cumming went through some periods in 'getting it there.'"

The Freund catalogue from 1951 lists the contents of the front hall as eighteenth-century portraits and Renaissance wrought-iron work, "XVIII Century Portraits and Renaissance Wrought Iron Work," specifically a "Renaissance grille serving as [a] door, XVI Century" and a "Hispano Moresque rhomboid trellis, partly gilded." The stair railing, rather than being that of a nineteenth-century brownstone, was early seventeenth-century Italian, "of the early XVII Century."

Tom remembers that on the ground floor, "there was the dining room, which was on your immediate left, and that had a Venetian boiserie that had very small pieces of glass in it and it was mercury glass, and theoretically it was before they even made glass in very large pieces." The Freund catalogue specifies "a complete Venetian rocaille mirrored dining room. Carved wood mullioned mirrors and floral decoration." The catalogue dates the mirrored boiserie to between 1725 and 1730 and reminds us that it had belonged to "Mrs. Richard Fellows of London," that is Daisy Fellows, the Singer sewing machine heiress and sometime editor of French *Vogue*, a provenance much loved by Rose.

Tom continued:

[There was] a big sled in the bay window ... No curtains ... And that [i.e. the sled] had all kinds of big huge magnolia leaves ... All candles were black. Always black...And then she had spotlights on the floor, and they had blue gels over them. I mean this is all way ahead of its time ... And that was back where the sled was and in the corners.

LEFT Rose's "Ugly Room," with the grotesque images and objects, predatory birds and beasts, and sinister paintings she had found over the years, all of which worked together comfortably.
Photograph by Harold Haliday Costain, Dessin Fournir Collections.

177

The catalogue identified the sled as *an extraordinary sleigh of the Regence [1715–1728], made in Alsace-Lorraine by a craftsman of [the city of] Nancy for Stanislas Lescinsky, the father-in-law of Louis XV. Carved in wood in a design of flamboyant Rocaille scrolls; lined in gold lamé brocade. Polychromed wrought-iron mounts and trough. Perhaps the most distinguished example of its kind in this country.*

The catalogue lists many more pieces of furniture with impressive provenances. Tom goes on to mention Rose's private stairway to the parlor floor of the house and the hallway on that floor. "The hall on the second floor had a chandelier that hung from it that was a huge ship made of crystal…with sails. A great big vessel and, you know, rather great fantasy to it, and then there were huge Chinese statues of goddesses carved in white marble."

ABOVE A sleigh that stood in Rose's dining room, filled with magnolia leaves. It dates to the Regence period in France, eighteenth century. *Photograph by Chuck Plante.*

RIGHT
Rose's dining room in the days before she had covered the walls with the mercury glass mirrors set with rosettes that came from Daisy Fellows. Rose later made into a chandelier the Venetian crystal ship that is a centerpiece here. The walls are akin to the jade green washed with Prussian blue that she painted her library. The Regence sleigh filled with magnolia leaves was a fixture, and the shadows on the walls came from the spotlights covered with blue gels that Thomas Britt called "ahead of their time."
Dessin Fournir Collections.

A hallway in Rose's house with a Chinese sculpted figure and a checked marble floor. *Dessin Fournir Collections.*

The hall on Rose's parlor floor with the crystal ship chandelier, a pair of Indo-Chinese statues of dancers, and a bronze Chinese pagoda. *Dessin Fournir Collections.*

Rose's library was distinguished by a crystal chandelier and red lacquer Venetian chairs set against the sea green walls, about which everyone commented.
Photograph by Harold Haliday Costain, courtesy of Keith de Lellis Gallery, New York.

The library with the jade-green walls that were washed with Prussian blue, the purple satin sofa, and the red lacquer chairs, all of which Mark Hampton said both "clashed admirably" and "had a mellow softness." *Courtesy of Sarah Cumming Cecil.*

RIGHT Rose's bedroom with a Portuguese iron bed, hung with silver lamé, blue foil wallpaper, and Venetian mirrored pelmets over silver curtains from Dazian, the theatrical costuming house. *Courtesy of Sarah Cumming Cecil.*

BELOW A nineteenth-century Thai or Burmese daybed that Rose used as a low table in her bedroom. After her death, Doris Duke bought it to add to her collection of Thai art, and upon her death it went to the Asian Art Museum of San Francisco. *Gift from Doris Duke Charitable Foundation's Southeast Asian Art Collection, 2006.27.51. © Asian Art Museum of San Francisco. Used by permission.*

An upstairs room in Rose's house distinguished by a
Knole sofa and a lampshade with cabalistic symbols.
*Photograph by Harold Haliday Costain, courtesy of
Keith de Lellis Gallery. New York.*

Stairway wall murals suggesting ancient
Chinese landscape paintings.
*Photograph by Harold Haliday Costain,
Dessin Fournir Collections.*

The catalogue identifies these figures as an early eighteenth century pair of Indo-Chinese marble dancers, probably attendants of Quan Yin (the Chinese goddess of mercy). There was also a Chinese bronze pagoda in the hallway; an eighteenth-century bronze urn holding the tree of life, whose branches bore gilded tole apples; and a "pre-Chippendale" eighteenth-century English aviary—"perhaps the most enchanting bird house in America," said the catalogue. Rose, in her 1928 *Arts & Decoration* article, talked about the tree of life with the tole apples: "The sacred Chinese apple tree in the Ming period tempts all comers with its harvest of luscious golden fruit. Like the tree in the garden of the Hesperides [which] Hercules plundered, but my apples are better guarded for there are two raging dragons instead of one to threaten the offender, although they are but of Chinese porcelain." (She is perhaps referring to the figures of the dancers or to statues of Foo dogs, which she later had in her garden.)

The hallway opened into the famous drawing room with its eighteenth-century silver figured Chinese wallpaper and mirrored doors. "It was really a drawing room," says Tom. "It did not have comfortable furniture in it. Not lounging furniture. She liked to be daring—no real floor plans." The wallpaper was probably installed some time in the 1930s, since it is not in the photographs from 1928. The Freund catalogue describes it as eighteenth century Chinese and "a most colorful and romantic wall cover…Decorated in tempera with trees, blossoms, birds and figures. This extraordinary paper covers the entire room. Family inheritance descending from the famous Earl of Bath, an early ambassador to the Emperor of China." Like many of Rose's provenances, this is more wishful than accurate, as the eighteenth-century Earl of Bath (who died without issue), while he was a political figure, never went to China.

On the other hand, the paper is undoubtedly eighteenth century Chinese and unbelievably scintillating in its silvery magic. At the same time, the accuracy of the statement about the origin of the chaise longue and bergère that break the space in the middle of the room carries conviction: "Early Louis Quinze. Stamped: 'P. Bara.' Pierre Bara entered the Corporation [that is, the guild of furniture makers] in 1758 and was celebrated as a chair maker. Recorded in Salverte: 'Les Ebenistes du 18ieme siecle.' 1927."

OPPOSITE Rose's exquisitely cluttered dressing table. *Photograph by G. W. Harting, Dessin Fournir Collections.*

There was a music room at one end of the drawing room, which contained a fruitwood spinet c.1795, and the library with the blue-green walls, where Rose entertained Albert Hadley, at the other end. Tom Britt says, "there were mirrored doors at each end of the [drawing] room—just slabs of mirror...the library was where the mirrored doors of the other end [of the drawing room] opened into, but she always had those closed because on the other side of those doors... there was a half of a coromandel screen."

Rose explains in her 1928 article how she achieved the color of the blue-green walls of the library, which are remembered lyrically by everyone—Albert Hadley, Mark Hampton, and Thomas Britt. "I used a real jade green for the walls of the library...Its exact shade can only be produced by the use of a certain very vivid green washed over with Prussian blue." Tom Britt says, "That's how you do it. Put one coat over another."

Moving upstairs, Tom recalls:

[I]t was rather odd the way you would enter her 'virgin lair' as she referred to her bedroom as well as the shop…. Rose called the guest room her mother's room.'

[But] when I was upstairs, her mother was already dead, so this is in the late 1950s, and you walked through her mother's room [to get to Rose's room]. [Her mother's room] was all in these beautiful mauves and lilacs and the whole bed with those ruffles and curtains and then the [window] curtains [were] one of her chintzes and then a polished floor and a lot of Louis XVI furniture in there.

The bed in Rose's mother's room was a *lit a polonaise*, an eighteenth-century style in which the canopy was gathered up to a central cluster of fabric.

Tom continues:

[Rose's] bedroom had these wonderful walls of a silver blue foil. She had bought that in London. It was a wrapping paper or something that she saw, according to what I've heard. And she put that on all the walls and then the ceiling was painted kind of misty—like clouds. And then she had three Venetian pelmets of mirror over the three windows, and she went to Dazian, which sold theatrical gauze and stuff [and which is still in business], and

that's what the curtains were made of…that's how she had those shimmering silvery curtains on the windows.

Mark Hampton, as we said earlier, remembers the bedroom walls as being the color and texture of the paper "on the box of a bottle of 'Evening in Paris' perfume."

Tom further says, "The Spanish iron bed was quite extraordinary." (The Freund catalogue says it was "Portuguese—XVIII Century.") Silver lamé was draped over the four posts, as well as hung at the windows; and Tom remembers that it was "really heavy. You could feel the weight when you put it in your hand. And I put that on the bed for her more than once, because she always liked to keep everything clean, so then it would pool on the floor at the foot of [the bed]."

Rose's garden, behind the house, was as magical as the house itself. A note written in the early 1950s to thank Rose for a dinner party mentions how delightful it was to "sit in your lovely garden." Thomas Britt says "the garden was fabulous… it had all Chinese furniture and mother of pearl, and I used to take her to a place to buy water plants." He also remembers that:

there were two huge Foo dogs that sat in this garden, and they were on top of pedestals. They were Ming [dynasty], so she said. When they were building Toots Shor['s Restaurant on the street behind her], they knocked the wall down and [the Foo dogs] fell, so she had a fit. She was very upset needless to say. I don't know why she had Ming statues out in the garden…but who would think they were going to knock the wall down?

Rose's house was undoubtedly her masterwork and no one who ever saw it forgot it. Her sense of color, her mannerist liking for beautiful things that were just a bit different, her sense of scale, and her sense of glamour all came together and created a shifting, glimmering experience. As her nephew, Russell Cecil, said, "the experience [of going from room to room] changed drastically as the colors changed."

Rose herself said as early as her article of 1928, "You asked me how long it took me to complete my house? I will answer that with a question. Is a house ever quite finished?"

OPPOSITE The garden behind Rose's Fifty-third Street house was a place of enchantment. Thomas Britt remembers Chinese furniture and mother-of-pearl and he would drive Rose to buy water plants for the fountain. *Photograph by Harold Haliday Costain, courtesy of Keith de Lellis Gallery. New York.*

"This extraordinary room was created by Rose Cumming as the result of a spur-of-the-moment reaction against the usual conception of prettiness in decorating. Sinister, ugly, destructive, or macabre objects and decorations are used, yet so skillfully and colorfully that a dramatic effect is created, as well as a room where a man could live and be comfortable."

Katharine Tweed, editor of *The Finest Rooms* (1964)

OPPOSITE Rose's "Ugly Room" with the wall of Audubon prints of predatory birds and animals. *Photograph by Harold Haliday Costain, courtesy of Keith de Lellis Gallery, New York.*

CHAPTER TEN

The Ugly Room

Mario Buatta, like Thomas Britt and Albert Hadley before him, walked into Rose's shop when he was a young man.

I remember the first time I went into her shop was when she was on Madison Avenue at 515, one shop up from the corner, and it was a deep entrance. You had to walk in, and I walked in and she didn't like the looks of me and she was sweeping. She said, "Young man—out with you! Out with you!" And she swept me right out of the shop …[T]hen we got to know each other somehow.

He goes on to tell how he, Tom Britt, Mark Hampton, and other young men, who were all friends, became friends of Rose. There is a snapshot, taken at a party given by Albert Hadley during those days. Rose, wearing her signature big-brimmed Adrian hat, is standing between Mark Hampton and Edward Lee Cave, who worked for Parish Hadley and later became a real estate magnate, and she is laughing. She looks frail and a little vulnerable, but as though she is having fun. It is very different from the image of the forbidding dragon shown in more formal photographs.

Mario Buatta tells how Rose would marshal her young men to come and clean her house on Saturdays. This is 30 years after the house first appeared in *Arts & Decoration*, so it must have been a little worn.

Mario says,

I was about 25, I think—yes, because it was when I was saving money to go to Europe. We got paid ten dollars and dinner. The dining room was on the first floor. Black floor, mirrored walls all antiqued and faded out and a blue slate ceiling so it looked like the most wonderful Venetian water. It was great.

OPPOSITE
A table set by Rose with
polished coal as the
centerpiece.
Dessin Fournir Collections.

ABOVE AND OPPOSITE
A party given by Albert Hadley in the early 1960s. Rose, in
typical colorful mode, is flirting for all she is worth with the late
Mark Hampton and Edgar Lee Cave, both of whom worked
at the time for Hadley and Sister Parish. These are among the
very few photographs in which Rose looks relaxed and happy.
Photograph by Albert Hadley, courtesy of Albert Hadley.

And she would be in the kitchen fixing dinner, which was pretty much cans of tuna fish and those little cherry tomatoes that she put in a skillet and simmered and whatever and then peas from the frozen packets but the color would be running off the peapods. She rapidly moved from kitchen to the pantry to the dining room, and one time she trips and goes "Whoops! Luckily we cleaned today." She scooped up the peas, and we had to sit there and eat them. So she was funny. She was odd. But she was terrific.

The flower and symbol of Rose's increasing eccentricity, as well as of her talent, in those years was the so-called Ugly Room at the top of her house. Tom Britt's former wife, Julie, says that Tom helped put Rose's "Ugly Room" together, although since Tom did not get to know Rose until the late 1950s, it's likely she had begun it earlier. In any case, she had certainly been collecting the components of it for decades. It represented the dark side of her unique personality, and also — always a consideration with Rose — her sense of humor. Mark Hampton describes the Ugly Room on the occasion of his first visit to Rose's house in 1962, accompanied by Albert Hadley: "On the third floor there was a sitting room, the walls of which were decorated with prints of snakes and reptiles, all, as Rose said, of a predatory nature, with more purple and silver…"

Katharine Tweed, editor of *The Finest Rooms* (1964), says this about the Ugly Room:

This extraordinary room was created by Rose Cumming as the result of a spur-of-the-moment reaction against the usual conception of prettiness in decorating. Sinister, ugly, destructive, or macabre objects and decorations are used, yet so skillfully and colorfully that a dramatic effect is created, as well as a room where a man could live and be comfortable.

Interesting that with all the wildlife in the room and its somewhat threatening atmosphere, its character is determined by Miss Tweed to be masculine, as opposed to the distinctly feminine character of the ruffled bedrooms below.

Dominating the Ugly Room was a painting by Jean Baptiste Oudry, a French painter who worked in the first half of the eighteenth century and who became known for his gnarled and sinister hunting scenes and still lifes. This particular

RIGHT The bronze Ming dynasty monkey, foreground, the harem doors from India across the windows, and the warrior's head from New Ireland on top of the bookcase were all displayed in the "Ugly Room." *Courtesy of Sarah Cumming Cecil.*

painting was limned by Miss Tweed as having been "painted in his black period, depicting a deep pool with wild ducks and a vulture poised for attack."

Above the couch in the Ugly Room there were Audubon prints of rats, weasels, and other creatures of prey; plates from an old book on venomous snakes embellished the tiles around the fireplace. A vase of early Spanish swords stood next to a toy leather boar, which was a seventeenth-century gout stool; and on a side table three-dimensional green reptiles writhed across a majolica plate. An Indonesian parasol had been turned into a lamp, and bronze Ming monkeys, as well as white porcelain Meissen monkeys, flanked the Knole sofa. Old saris veiled the windows, which were covered with harem doors from India. A vicious-looking carved warrior's head from New Ireland glared at the room from the top of the bookcase. Cyclamen pink tufts of wool enlivened the seventeenth-century Corsican rugs.

The Ugly Room in the early 1960s, when Mark Hampton and Mario Buatta experienced it, foreshadowed an ugly time in Rose's life. In the late 1950s, Rose lost her shop at 515 Madison Avenue, after more than 25 years, and not long afterward, in the mid-1960s, she sold her West Fifty-third Street House, where she had been since the 1920s. These were the theaters for her performances of creativity and the mainstays of her life. The block of Fifty-third Street where her house stood, just across the street from the Museum of Modern Art, was being extensively redeveloped by the time she left. The Donnell branch of the New York Public Library had opened just to the east of her in 1955; and at the corner of Fifty-third Street and Fifth Avenue, the monolithic, aluminum-clad Tishman Building, known as "666" because of its sinister address, which was emblazoned across the top in scarlet letters, opened in 1957. In 1965, the 38-story CBS headquarters, designed by Eero Saarinen and known as "Black Rock" because of its inky stone facade, opened at the other end of the block.

Rose moved her shop, backed by Eileen, as always, and Dorothy, whose design shops and fabric businesses—for which she used Rose as an outlet—were flourishing in Jamaica. Rose was able to relocate to what Mario Buatta describes as a car showroom at Park Avenue and Fifty-ninth Street. The

LEFT The eighteenth-century painting by Jean Baptiste Oudry, with the threatened wildlife, the venomous snakes on the tiles around the fireplace, and the Indonesian parasol lampshade added sinister depths to the "Ugly Room." *Photograph by Harold Haliday Costain, courtesy of Keith de Lellis Gallery, New York.*

space had windows 30 feet high, which Rose loved, and she soon stocked it with her alluring and unforgettable mixture of the very old, the very valuable, and the very beautiful, put together with whimsy and junk.

Mark Hampton remembers in *Legendary Decorators of the Twentieth Century* that he first met Rose

on a suffocatingly hot August afternoon in 1962 … Walking up Park Avenue, I stopped in front of Rose's shop, which I had never seen before, to gaze at the arresting conglomeration of furniture, objects, and bolts of old chintz that filled her windows. Hanging in the center was a big, rusty iron chandelier, casually and rather messily draped with crystal. Whole areas of this very delicate and beautiful chandelier were devoid of any prisms or beads, while other branches were laden with too many strands, some hanging down like old cobwebs. It was covered with dust and seemed completely unsuitable for any customer. It was nevertheless divine in its weird way. Peeking past the oddities in the window, I saw a solitary, elderly figure with electrified blue hair standing out like a nimbus around her head. Finding the door around the corner, I knocked cautiously and stepped inside, to begin what turned out to be a long conversation and an even longer friendship with Rose, one of the most eccentric and original people I've ever known.

Hampton, who was sometimes part of the cleaning crew with Mario Buatta and Thomas Britt, went occasionally on his own to help.

She lived in this large brownstone, completely alone, with no help. So on Saturdays we would polish floors or I would move large pieces of furniture and try to get to the high, out-of-reach places that she, at her age and by herself, was unable to do. On one of these Saturdays, another hot summer afternoon, I had gone, armed with a large bottle of Windex, to polish the walls of the famous Daisy Fellowes dining room. Rose, with her typical joie de vivre, in celebration of the newly sparkling room, insisted on going to the pantry and rummaging around for a tin of caviar, which we opened (I had never tasted it before in my life). We sat there, eating caviar and drinking Scotch with no ice, another example of her Anglophilia. This playful, generous quality, having a great time cleaning, eating caviar, and laughing was quintessential Rose.

Her rooms, which were beautiful, mysterious, sometimes even a little weird, and full of risky decorating practices, had a wonderful quality of wit and humor.

Mark Hampton's wife, Duane, says that when she met Rose, a few years after Mark's cleaning stints, "Rose was funny and immediately friendly. We sat on the stoop eating disgusting caviar…She reminded me of an American Madeleine Castaing. She taught Mark so much."

Rose with her young protégés, who cleaned her house and took her to the movies, enjoyed a last autumnal flowering in her life. She still held her iconic place in the design world. As late in her life as 1964, she was one of a dozen designers asked to create place settings for Tiffany, and 1964 also saw the publication of *The Finest Rooms*, edited by Katharine Tweed of Viking Press. This volume has a lovely and penetrating essay by Rose, with photographs of her work, along with the work of other designers who defined the profession, such as Billy Baldwin, Eleanor Brown of McMillen, and Sister Parish.

Despite these accolades, Rose's life was blurring, and the eccentricity was poking out in awkward, jagged ways. Now there were stories of Rose going out to hale a taxi wearing a fur coat with nothing under it. When young men were sent from the fabric companies to retrieve fabrics that Rose had kept for months or even years on approval, they would be summoned into a back room where Rose was stretched on a chaise longue wearing very little clothing. It was as though, having lived a life of flirtation, Rose had no other way to validate her existence.

These were the days after Rose had sold her house on Fifty-third Street. With the money, she bought an apartment on upper Fifth Avenue and decorated it, at least partly, with her usual panache. The dining room had black lacquered walls with tulle netting swagged across them in which sequins had been scattered. Rose never lived there, however. After a lifetime of braving it alone, she felt the wind of mortality too strongly and she was too confused. She lived with the widowed Eileen, who also had an apartment on Fifth Avenue.

OPPOSITE The drawing room of interior designer Thomas Britt's New York house featuring the collection of Audubon prints of predatory birds that once hung in Rose's "Ugly Room."
Photograph by Jeffrey Hirsch, courtesy of the New York Social Diary.

Albert Hadley tells the story of Rose coming to a dinner party at Sister Parish's (whom she had gotten to know through the good offices of Albert) in the 1960s. She was wearing a green satin gown hiked up with a gold curtain cord and she had a wreath of green plastic leaves in her hair. The doorman did not want to let her in. A poignant finale for the Rose who, as a belle of the 1920s, was recorded as "looking too beautiful in a lavender satin gown with a green wreath around her hair" and whom "everybody wanted to meet."

Rose still lived in her own time as her world crumbled.

New York designer Bunny Williams remembers meeting Rose at the very end of her life and at the beginning of what would be a stellar career for Bunny:

This was about 1966, because I was 20 years old when I came to work at Stair & Company. It was my first job in New York, and of course in those days, you know, Fifty-seventh Street had all the

great shops—they sold French furniture, there was the Antique Porcelain Company, it was "the place"—if you wanted Marie Antoinette's table, that's where you went. Stair & Company had English furniture, all very sedate, but around the corner there was this magic window that we would all walk by. I was 20 or 21 years old, and every night I would leave Stair & Company, and I would walk up and I would look in the window of this shop. It was just like nothing you had ever seen.

Finally, after a year and a half, I was walking home one day, and the lights were on, and I went in and introduced myself. Rose Cumming was there and quite frumpy—you know, this frizzy purplish blue hair, not particularly chicly dressed and just wandering around this fabulous shop. I said to her, "I'm working at Stair & Company, and I've looked in your window for a year and a half, and I just had to come in, and I can't afford to buy anything!" She was so sweet. She actually looked me over, and she locked the door, and she said, "Well, it's the end of the day." And

RIGHT Rose in a relatively mellow mood, wearing one of her signature low cut dresses. *Photograph by Albert Hadley, courtesy of Albert Hadley.*

Fashion designer Bill Blass used Rose Cumming fabrics in some of his evening gowns. Here the skirt is "Cumming Rose" and the bodice is made of cutwork roses.
Courtesy of Bill Blass Fashions, LLC.

she spent several hours talking with me. It was fabulous! Here was this mirrored glass wall, and she got out the hand blocked chintzes and the "Banana Leaf." What was so astounding about her taste was that it was so off the wall. I mean it was reptiles, and there was a sort of Hollywood chic to it, but then there was sort of this macabre thing going on, and none of it was consistent, but they were things you had never seen before…she puttered around, bringing things off the shelves and talking about hand blocked fabrics and the chintzes, which you just don't see anymore in these purple backgrounds and blue backgrounds, and explaining the process. The shop was a mess. Really it was dirty, and the silver gilt furniture and the big mirrored wall—! Certainly coming from working in a shop where everything was prim and proper and eighteenth century, as I was, this was decoration that you just knew you were very drawn to.

It was evident to Bunny that Rose was failing.

She was kind of a little dotty at that time, but I thought it was so nice of her to take a young person who was interested and walk around and talk in the shop. I had always been afraid to go into the shop, because there was something rather menacing about it. The windows weren't exactly styled in a way that was inviting, but once you got in it was just something "magical!"

Bunny was entranced by Rose's fabrics, both the very old ones and the ones that Rose said she had commissioned.

They did no machine printing at that time [when Rose was working with fabrics]. If you go and buy old curtains and they're hand blocked, there's such a difference—it's like painting versus just rolled out [with a printer], and the definition of colors [is so strong], and of course the older fabrics had all these bizarre colors in them. I mean they would be on a royal blue background, but they had sort of puce [with it], and, you know, weird funny colors, which is really what made them exciting, and I think we've lost that. The colorists have lost that ability to use the kind of bright colors with the weird colors. It was amazing. [There were] purple and chartreuse and, of course, in those days in that time decorating was very "powder blue dining rooms." The color revolution hadn't started. So to go into her shop and see it was phenomenal.

As a designer, what I am going to look at in Rose's work is this extraordinary use of color and the unusual furniture. It certainly makes you look at things in a different way. You took away something that was very magical and took more chances and were more daring because you had seen it and had been in the shop.

Rose died in 1968 and her last few years were chaotic and miserable. Bunny Williams, one of the few of Rose's acquaintances who imagined her life from the inside, instead of seeing her as a character performing for others, thinks Rose must have been lonely and that "life must have been tough for her." In the end, the long-suffering Eileen not only had Rose living with her, but also their half sister, Marge, the poor relation from Australia, who by this time was in a wheelchair. Marge's granddaughter remembers spending the night there as a child. "Rose had satin sheets, and I had to wash my feet before I got into bed. Rose was fun," she says. "My grandmother was not fun." There are some snapshots of Rose at Eileen's country house on Long Island, looking skeletal but wearing one of her signature big hats and still gamely raising a glass of champagne. Then there is one in which she just stares sadly and vacantly into the camera.

Following Rose's death, there was an auction of her inventory and personal effects on October 23, 1968, at Parke Bernet, the old New York auction house that was to merge with Sotheby's. Rose's penchant for mingling with celebrities extended beyond the grave—the two auctions that took place ahead of hers contained the personal effects of Edna Ferber, the best-selling novelist, and Elizabeth Arden, the cosmetics queen. Rose's possessions were spread over two auctions: the morning session offered "Decorative and Table Porcelain," which included Coalport, Staffordshire, Sevres, Paris, Berlin, and Chinese. There were also "Works of Art and Other Decorations," including framed prints, lamps and Oriental screens. The afternoon session offered furniture and more substantial pieces, including four more screens. Our old friend from Fifty-third Street, the "Hispano Moresque Wrought Iron Gate" which guarded Rose's front

door, was also among these pieces. Although a few unrelated items were added at the end of Rose's auctions, her goods were the lion's share. The total sale for the morning auction was $9435; the afternoon fetched $29,342.50.

Rose's legacy lived on in a number of ways. Fashion designer Bill Blass used Rose's fabrics for some of his evening dresses. The decision was made to continue with the shop and Eileen took it over, operating it later with Ronald Grimaldi, who put the business on a sound footing. The traditions of style and generosity continued.

Oscar de la Renta remembers that he used to walk home from his work at Elizabeth Arden past Rose's store every night, and that one night he saw this fantastic secretary desk, made of mother-of-pearl and tortoiseshell, with an inside of marquetry and bone. He was at a dinner party at Babe Paley's house the following evening, and Babe told him that she had seen the same piece in the store, had fallen in love with it, and had inquired as to the price, but it turned out to be too expensive for her. Oscar then said to himself that if it was too expensive for Babe Paley, it would be too expensive for him, as he was very early in his career at this point. Two weeks later, however, after seeing the desk every night, he told himself that he was in love with it, and that he had to have it. He went into the store and spoke to Rose Cumming's sister and asked how much the desk was. He was told it was $25,000. He told her that it was impossible for him to pay that, asked what her best price was, and if he could pay over time. He bought the desk for $22,000 and paid it off over three years. Every month he gave what he could from his paycheck, sometimes more, sometimes less. He was never harassed no matter how little he gave that month. The secretary is in Oscar de la Renta's house in the Dominican Republic to this day.

ABOVE Ronald Grimaldi and Eileen in the shop. Grimaldi came to work with Eileen after Rose's death and revived the sale of fabrics, putting it on sound footing. *Photograph by Peter Vitale.*

RIGHT
One of the last photographs of Rose shows her emaciated but gamely raising a glass in her Adrian hat.
Courtesy of Sarah Cumming Cecil.

In the end, Bunny Williams has the last word in one of the greatest tributes that Rose, as both designer and mentor, would ever receive.

"I think she freed up all of us to take more chances."

OPPOSITE The drawing room showing the papier-mâché Venetian chandelier and chinoiserie Chippendale mirror over the fireplace. Also displayed is Rose's helter-skelter sense of furniture placement, which she described as "pushing it around until it was right."
Courtesy of Sarah Cumming Cecil.

EPILOGUE

CHARLES COMEAU, CEO AND CO-FOUNDER
THE DESSIN FOURNIR COLLECTIONS

Rose Cumming Today

When the Dessin Fournir Collections acquired the Rose Cumming fabric and wall covering line in 2005, people questioned why. We already had a successful textile firm, Classic Cloth.

We admired Rose Cumming because she was one of the bastions of design and represented the best of New York in a time that no longer exists. Our companies are constant advocates for preserving history and a tradition of doing business as Rose founded it. We saw the history that Rose and her fabrics embodied and wanted to carry on her legacy. In everything from her personal flamboyance to her innovative use of color and strong sense of discipline, we saw Rose Cumming as being as relevant today as she was when she started in 1921.

We looked ahead to see where Rose Cumming was going. If Rose were still here today, what would she be doing? Luckily for us, Rose created more designs than she was able to produce and we discovered a treasure trove of documents and inspirations among her archives. These archives afforded many opportunities to advance and develop new products for the line with the flair and élan that Rose was known for.

When you look at the color scheme of her wallpapers and fabrics, you see elegance, simplicity and a palette that pushes the envelope like no other. Her color work alone proves that Rose was, and still is, ahead of her time. Just to look through her design file folders excites the senses and boggles the mind. She was so forward thinking in her use of color, texture, techniques and application that photographs hardly do her work justice.

A prolific designer, Rose always created with variety. The rich, vibrant quality of her prints came from her skillful layering of color. We even discovered old documents that Rose did in muted colors—beige, grisaille, tan, lavender and soft greens. There was not a hue that Rose could not master.

Today, we are in the process of bringing Rose's design sense into the next century, safeguarding her signature designs and color work while continuously innovating in her honor, expanding her legacy to future generations, hoping to keep Rose forever in bloom.

Jeremiah Goodman's evocation of Rose's mother's room.
Painting by Jeremiah Goodman, courtesy of Dean Morgan.

The prince and his bride rented
an apartment in Rose's house.
It ended badly with the prince
suing Rose for "failure to provide
services." Jeremiah Goodman
said, "Rose couldn't have cared
less." She won the lawsuit.

THE BROWNSTONE HOUSE OF ROSE CUMMING
36 West 53rd Street
New York

People from all over the country have frequently asked Rose Cumming, the renowned decorator, how she lived, what were her predelictions, what sort of art objects did she care for and keep for herself for constant companions, and they have often asked her to let them go through her house and garden to find out the guiding inspiration of her life after business hours.

Until now it has only been feasible to invite friends and a few strangers whose houses she had furnished.

More and more frequently Rose Cumming has been urged by Museum directors and curators, as well as by prominent educators, to open her house for inspection to the public and she has now yielded to these friendly suggestions.

The main purpose of this brochure is to serve as a brief catalogue of the highlights of what the visitor can expect to see and study for beauty of line and color, as well as historic appeal. The objects in the following paragraphs are picked at random among the hundreds of fascinating and aristocratic objects of arts and crafts which are inhabitants of these beautiful rooms. We call them inhabitants because they animate the interiors by their sheer presence. They all are thoroughbreds conveying imagination, good taste and pure architectural proportions, which are the artistic heritage of bygone centuries.

The House of Rose Cumming can boast with justification of its international atmosphere, of the fact that it brings centuries of artistry and artisanry together to create the perfect comfort of the home, free of the orthodox "period" imprisonment.

We cannot give a complete inventory of the contents of the house in this limited space, but here are some of the chapters of romance and history which the great craftsmen of old prophetically composed for Rose Cumming to take their rightly place in the interiors of lofty rooms, parquet floors and wonderful old mantel pieces, eighteen in number, framing open fireplaces, the natural, almost paternal, focus of any room.

To these objects of her choice she longs to come back after the arduous planning for the keenly appreciative American home lovers.

KARL FREUND

Admission $1.00
Please use garden entrance.

THE HOUSE OF ROSE CUMMING

<u>SOME OF THE HIGHLIGHTS</u>

<u>ENTRANCE HALL</u>: XVIII CENTURY PORTRAITS AND RENAISSANCE WROUGHT IRON WORK.

Pompeo Battoni (1708-1787) "Conversation Piece". Italian, XVIII Century.

Antoine Pesne (1683-1757) "Portrait of Joseph II as a Young Man".

Renaissance grille serving as door, XVI Century. Hispano Moresque rhomboid trellis, partly gilded.

Stair rail of the early XVII Century. Italian Renaissance.

<u>DINING ROOM</u>: EARLY GEORGIAN AND REGENCE FURNITURE AND DECORATIONS.

A complete Venetian Roccaille mirrored dining room. Carved wood mullioned mirrors and floral decoration. From the celebrated interiors of Mrs. Richard Fellows of London. Ca. 1725-1730.

Brescia marble mantel piece of the Regence. Early XVIII Century.

An extraordinary sleigh of the Regence, made in Alsace-Lorraine by a craftsman of Nancy for Stanislas Lescinsky, the father-in-law of Louis XV. Carved in wood in a design of flamboyant Roccaille scrolls; lined in gold lame brocade. Polychromed. Wrought iron mounts and trough. Perhaps the most distinguished example of it's kind in this country.

Carved oak console of the Regence period, by William Kent. Date, ca. 1740.

Model of a bambino cradle made for the House of Savoy. Italian XVIII Century. From the Tolentino Collection.

Crystal glass chandelier of extraordinary quality of the Regence period. Pendants of unmatched beauty. Early XVIII Century.

Pair of exceptional William Kent consoles of carved pine, with Indian head caryatids.

Authentic Boule table with lotus shaped top; exceptional mounts. Tortoise shell mosaics on top and apron. Early XVIII Century.

<u>2ND FLOOR HALL</u>: ORIENTAL AND ENGLISH ORNAMENTS OF THE XVIII CENTURY.

Pair of Indo-Chinese marble dancers. Probably attendants of Qwan Yin. Early XVIII Century.

Chinese bronze pagoda. Kang Hsi temple ornament.

XVIII Century bronze urn holding tree of life. From the branches are suspended gilded tole apples. Indo-Chinese.

Pre-Chippendale aviary. First quarter XVIII Century. Perhaps the most enchanting bird house in America.

MUSIC ROOM: XVIII CENTURY, ORIENTAL, CONTINENTAL AND ENGLISH FURNITURE, PAINTINGS and
              RARE BIBELOTS.

Two "sand" pictures. One representing a basket of flowers; the other a bowl with fruit
and flowers. The work of Benjamin Zobel (1815-1820) who worked in London during the
later days of George III and who claimed to have invented the process which he called
"marmo tinto" - tinted marble. This process employed marble dust. Benjamin Zobel was
a Suabian artist, who emigrated to England in the beginning of the XIX Century.

Goa (Indo-Portuguese) precious wood work table, inlaid with ivory. XVIII Century.
Anglo-Indian example of perfect taste.

Pair of six light wall brackets of the Adam period. Collection of the Duchess of
Sutherland (Lady Millicent Hawes).

Carrara marble mantel of the Adam period, carved with bas reliefs of Ceres and Flora.

Parquetry fruitwood spinet by Johan Emricus Senft, A.D.1795. Black and white keys in
perfect condition; the tone has an amazing resonance. Eastern French.

Music stand, painted in gold on black lacquer. Early Regency, ca. 1805. Probably
designed by Hope.

Fruitwood mosaic table with delicately ornamented top; naturalistically painted flowers.
Marbelized glazed inlays on apron.

Pair of half moon consoles of the Adam period in the French taste. XVIII Century.
Rich figured Kingwood veneer top.

Six light chandelier. Louis Seize, 3rd quarter XVIII Century. Believed to be the
work of a French craftsman for the Czarina of Russia.

Elaborate Venetian eglomise and blue glass mirror of the Regency period. Ca. 1730-1740.

Sir Henry Raeburn, R.C., Scottish, 1756-1823. "The Gage Children". From Collection of
Lord Leverhulme. A renowned group painting by the great Scotch master.

Pair of exquisite embroidered ivory and "marmo tinto" pictures. Anglo-Italian, Late
XVIII Century.

Amboyna wood childs writing desk. XVIII Century. A great rarity of cabinet makers
art.

Pair of exceptional Directoire chairs furnished with carved crossed arrows. Ca. 1800.
Collection of Sophie Schratt, the celebrated actress -- formerly in the Imperial
Austrian Collection (Castle of Schoenbrunn)

DRAWING ROOM: RARE FRENCH FURNITURE and ORIENTAL ART

Carved Chippendale console; most imaginative rusticated design. English, mid-XVIII
Century. From Phillips-Hitchin collection.

Chaise longue and bergere. Early Louis Quinze. Stamped: "P.Bara". Pierre Bara entered the Corporation in 1758 and was celebrated as a chair maker. Recorded in Salverte:
"Les Ebenistes du 18ieme siecle", 1927.

Outstanding Louis XV gueridon of tulipwood and rosewood. French, ca. 1760.

Set of nine French fauteuils bonne femme. Original lacquer. Ca. 1770. From the Lily
Havemeyer Collection.

A most colorful and romantic wall cover. Chinese, XVIII Century. Decorated in tempera with trees, blossoms, birds and figures. This extraordinary paper covers the entire room. Family inheritance descending from the famous Earl of Bath, an early Ambassador to the Emperor of China.

Pair of Sang de boeuf tapering cache pots. Yung Cheng, Early XVIII Century.

Fruitwood chess table; cabriole supports. XVIII Century. From Grenoble, probably by Hache.

Fine collection of antique Persian faiences.

Louis Quinze parquetry tulipwood ladies secretary. Original mounts. French, mid-XVIII Century.

Stuart carvings with Simian subjects by Effringham, the Elder, renowned wood carver of the period. End of the XVII Century. Collection Mrs. William K. Vanderbilt.

LIBRARY: ENGLISH FURNITURE, PORTRAITS and ART OBJECTS OF THE XVIII and EARLY XIX CENTURIES.

A magnificent Louis Quinze crystal glass chandelier with leaf shaped pendants and globular finial.

Sir William Beechey, R.A., British, 1753-1839. "Portrait of Admiral Maitland in red coat". He commanded the British ship which took Napoleon to the Island of Elba.

Portrait of a lady of rank. Bolognese school. Mid-XVIII Century. Superb carved and gilded wood frame of the Chippendale period.

Sir William Beechey, R.A. Original watercolor. Said to represent Thackeray and friends. Signed at the lower left.

Pair Chinese ceiling wax lacquer tables. XVIII Century.

Set of four crimson and gold lacquer Portuguese chairs. Mid-XVIII Century.

Carved Columnar Sienna, Fleur de peche and carrara mantel of the Adam period. English, XVIII Century.

Sir Archer Martin Shea: portrait believed to be the likeness of young Disraeli.

Georgeian furniture:
      Two mahogany Sheraton bookcases of distinguished design and warm patine.
      One small and graceful example of the Regency, a bookcase.

Pre-Chippendale chaise longue on cabriole supports -- of perfect proportion. Mid-XVIII Century.

Red lacquer secretary bookcase of the Queen Anne period, with mirrored doors. In remarkable state of preservation. Early XVIII Century.

3RD FLOOR ENTRANCE HALL

A varied collection of Chinese mirror pictures and animal sculptures. XVIII and early XIX Century.

GUEST BEDROOM: XVIII CENTURY FRENCH AND ENGLISH FURNITURE, PAINTINGS AND DECORATIONS.

Sir Allan Ramsay, Scottish, 1713-1784. Portrait of Lady Grant, in rose colored court dress. Contemporary frame.

Louis Seize mantel. Griotte and carved white marble. Pure classic design.

Louis Seize tester and canopied single bed.

French mahogany bouillotte gueridon of the XVIII Century.

Burl Elm wood desk of the Louis Seize period.

Oval Venetian mirror-mosaic, Murano glass; ornamented with flower wreaths in low relief. Gold ground. Louis Seize period.

HALLWAY

English satinwood spinet decorated by Angelica Kauffmann. Maker: Jas. Longman, London. Ca. 1780.

MASTER BEDROOM: ORIENTAL, RUSSIAN and ENGLISH ART, XVII and XVIII CENTURIES.

Two simian ceramics; one from Capo di Monte; the other from the Meissen factory.

Twelve fold Coromandel screen. of great importance. Kang Hsi. Maroon with gold ground enrichments.

Portuguese wrought iron tester bed with festooned drapery. XVIII Century. Indian bedspread of gold lame.

Pair of Chippendale carved and gilded mirrors, with the arms of the Earl of Stafford. Collection of Col. Harry Vernon of the Horse Guards.

Antique Chinese rugs of pale yellow.

Two silver stools and one silver table, made for the Russian Court. Ca. 1800.

Chippendale carved pine console. Third quarter XVIII Century. From the Phillips-Hitchin Collection.

Korean inlaid cabinet. Exquisite workmanship. Black and gold lacquer, inlaid with mother of pearl. XVIII Century.

James II red and gold lacquered cabinet. English, late XVII Century. Exceedingly rare.

1ST FLOOR; REAR HALL

Oriental Lowestoft porcelain set serving 36 people. Chinese late XVIII Century.

Pair of columnar consoles with elaborate mosaic marble tops. Mosaic panels on brocatelle marble ground.

Hispano Moorish Haremlik screen. XVI or XVII Century. Fruitwood. Andalusian.

PLAZA 8-0844 · 1029

Rose Cumming, INC.

SPECIALIST IN DECORATION
ANTIQUES, BIBELOTS
IMPORTED FABRICS
ANTIQUE WALLPAPERS

THE FINE ARTS BUILDING
232 EAST 59TH STREET
NEW YORK, N. Y. 10022

History of "Raindrop" Chandelier:

Rose Cumming found this chandelier while on a motor trip to Canada accompanied by three (3) European suitors — an Italian, a Russian and an Englishman. She owned a Lincoln touring car driven by her long-time chauffeur, Cole, who sat in the "pneumonia seat" — so-called because it was an uncovered space where the driver sat (in all kinds of weather) divided by a glass partition in which the passenger sat in the enclosed rear of the car and communicated with the chauffeur through a speaker-tube.

One afternoon, Rose Cumming spied an antiques shop where she found the rain-drop chandelier (so called because it looked like cascading rain drops formed out of crystal) and bought it on the spot. When asked if and how she'd like it sent to N.Y.

Rose Cumming, INC. 2

THE FINE ARTS BUILDING
232 EAST 59TH STREET
NEW YORK, N. Y. 10022

She replied adamantly that she would "take it with her now!" They tied it to the roof with twine and off they went on their expedition. Soon, thereafter, the automobile's horn went funny and Cole couldn't toot the horn! No problem for Miss Cumming. She had him stop at a local 5 & 10¢ store and bought a trumpet. She told him to tap on the window when he needed to toot the horn and she would roll-down the rear window and "sound the trumpet." Simple!?!

One can picture the scene — an eccentric woman with lavender hair being driven in an ancient touring car surrounded by three admirers, blowing a trumpet out the window with a crystal chandelier strapped to the roof! They wound their way back to New York and all ended well.

BIBLIOGRAPHY

Allen, Frederick Lewis. *Only Yesterday*. New York: Harper Perennial Modern Classics, 2010.

Arts & Decoration. New York: Chagnon & Company, March 1926; May 1928; July 1937.

Freund, Karl. Catalogue for Rose Cumming Collection. New York: Privately Printed, 1951.

Gura, Judith. *New York Interior Design 1935–1985: Inventors of Tradition*. New York: Acanthus Press Visual Library, 2008.

Hampton, Mark. *Legendary Decorators of the Twentieth Century*. New York: Doubleday, 1992.

House & Garden. New York: Condé Nast, April 1917; December 1927; July 1930.

Matz, Mary Jane. *The Many Lives of Otto Kahn*. New York: Macmillan, 1963.

Meyer, Gerald J. *A World Undone: The Story of the Great War 1914 to 1918*. New York: Random House, 2006.

Museum of Modern Art. *The Wind*. Program Review. New York: The Museum of Modern Art.

Sunday Mirror Magazine. London: *Sunday Mirror*, February 25, 1951.

Tweed, Katharine. *The Finest Rooms by America's Great Decorators*. New York: The Viking Press, 1964.

With the exception of miscellaneous facts and phrases taken from journals located in the New York Public Library or the Condé Nast Library, all of the material not attributed here either comes from personal interviews conducted by the author or from the Cecil Cumming family archives.

INDEX

Note: Page numbers in *italic* indicate illustrations.